AUTO CLAIMS WITHOUT ATTORNEYS
A Guide To Settlement

DOUG FITZPATRICK

Second Edition, Revised

COURTNEY PUBLISHING
SEDONA, ARIZONA

AUTO CLAIMS WITHOUT ATTORNEYS

A GUIDE TO SETTLEMENT

By Doug Fitzpatrick

Published by:

Courtney Publishing
49 Bell Rock Plaza
Sedona, AZ 86351
www.autojustice.net

First Printing 1998

Second Printing, 2001, revised

Printed in the United States of America

Library of Congress Cataloging-in-Publication Data
Fitzpatrick, Doug

Auto Claims Without Attorneys, A Guide to Settlement / by Doug Fitzpatrick – 2nd edition

Includes bibliographical references and index
ISBN 0-9712350-0-7

TABLE OF CONTENTS

APPENDIX

ABOUT THE AUTHOR

DOUGLAS C. FITZPATRICK

(928) 284-2190 • Fax 284-2191 • fitzlaw@sedona.net

49 BELL ROCK PLAZA SEDONA, ARIZONA 86351

EDUCATION

Lake Forest College, BA	1970
Chicago-Kent College of Law, JD	1975

BAR MEMBERSHIPS

State of Arizona Supreme Court	1977
United States District Court District of Arizona	1977

EXPERIENCE

Law Office of Douglas C. Fitzpatrick		
Owner	Sedona, Arizona	1982 - present
	Phoenix, Arizona	1977 - 1982
Phoenix College		
Adjunct faculty paralegal studies		1980 - 1982
Private investigator	Scottsdale, Arizona	1976 - 1977
	Lake County, Illinois	1974 – 1976
Lake County (Illinois) Public Defender		1975
Lake County (Illinois) Juvenile Court		1972 - 1974
McHenry County (Illinois) Juvenile Court		1970 – 1972

In the 24 years Mr. Fitzpatrick has been licensed to practice law in Arizona's state and federal courts, he has tried hundreds of cases. In addition, he has represented numerous clients whose cases have settled without litigation. The emphasis of Mr. Fitzpatrick's practice has been in the personal injury arena.

CONTINUING LEGAL EDUCATION

Trial Skills: The Closing Argument	1990
Damages: For Plaintiff and Defense Attorneys in Arizona	1992
The Permanency of Whiplash	1996
Insurance Coverage Law in Arizona	1996
Adjusting the Automobile Injury Claim in Arizona	1996
Settlement Conferences and Mediation	1997
Trying the Automobile Injury Case in Arizona	1999
Medical Records for Arizona Attorneys	2000
Advanced Personal Injury Practice in Arizona	2000
Premises Liability: Preparation and Trial of a Difficult Case in Arizona	2000
2001 Alternate Dispute Resolution	2001
Pilot Arbitration Training	2001

PUBLICATIONS

"The Attorney's Duty to Reduce the Contingent Fee: *In the Matter of Swartz Revisited,*" Arizona Attorney, Feb. 1999 pp. 18-19.

ACKNOWLEDGEMENT

I acknowledge my wife, Nancy, and daughters, Priscilla and Courtney. It was their tragic auto accident of November 11, 1998, which put into motion a series of events, including a lawsuit, which has been difficult for all of us. This book is spawned in part by the adversity of that process and, I trust, will be among the good things which have come out of our challenges.

To my faithful assistant, Marilyn Miller, I am grateful for her extra time and effort with word-processing, formatting, and other tedious detail work which added to her already full plate managing my law practice.

Thanks, Lois Kay, for helping out with the document preparation. I'm grateful that you've been able to fill in for Marilyn when we've needed you. You've become a key part of our team.

I acknowledge Richard Carmen, a friend and fellow author, whose encouragement to get on with this project has motivated me to write this manual.

And thanks to Alan Aufrance and Kate Bosman of PSR Advertising for excellent work in the cover design, graphics, and marketing.

CAUTION

This book has been written by an attorney to guide consumers through the automobile claims process in routine cases. It may reduce the need for legal representation in cases when an attorney is not needed on a full time basis. One of the objectives of the book is to save the consumer money by minimizing the involvement of attorneys in auto claims.

It is not the purpose of this manual to reprint all the information that's available to the author concerning auto claims. You are urged to read all the relevant material, learn as much as possible about the claims process and tailor the information in this book to your specific needs.

Settling an auto claim without an attorney is not a way to get rich. Anyone who would settle his or her own claim should invest the necessary time and effort reading and understanding this book and the materials referred to in it. For claims involving serious injuries and/or troublesome liability or insurance coverage issues, the services of a competent attorney should be sought.

Every effort has been made to make this manual as complete and accurate as possible. However, laws and procedures change frequently and are subject to differing interpretations. Therefore, this text should be used only as a general guide and not as the ultimate source of information concerning the auto claims process. If you want legal advice backed by a guarantee, see a lawyer.

The author and publisher shall have no liability to any person with respect to any loss or damage alleged to be caused, directly or indirectly, by the information contained in this book.

If you do not wish to be bound by the above, you may return this book to the publisher for a full refund.

PREFACE

This book was written to fill a need for information about the auto claims process. It's a consumer guide for anyone who would navigate the auto claims minefield without turning over all the control and much of the recovery to an attorney. It will empower you to negotiate on a level playing field with the insurance adjuster.

Notwithstanding the title, **AUTO CLAIMS *WITHOUT* AN ATTORNEY**, the objective is not to remove attorneys from the claims process in all cases. The book offers practical guidance with respect to when and how to use an attorney. Even with the routine cases, strategic but limited use of an attorney is encouraged. The goal is to avoid paying 30% to 40% of the recovery in legal fees when it's not necessary.

This book is also a call for reform of the legal system, parts of which are badly in need of repair. Many attorneys acknowledge that they have an image problem. Skepticism about lawyers and attorney jokes are symptomatic of the low regard which many have for the profession.

Most lawyers would attribute the black eye they seem to have suffered to the "few bad apples" who get more publicity than they deserve. After all, the attorneys ask, don't many professions have their few practitioners who seem to want to give their colleagues a black eye? This rationalization underestimates the seriousness of the plight which has befallen the lawyers.

I've taken freedom in directing criticism at the profession of which I have been a part for almost twenty-five years. I trust that this book will be of value to the many people who need guidance when caught up in the auto claims process. If the criticism of attorneys and the fee system they control brings about debate, discussion, and reform, that's better yet.

"It is a rough road that leads to the heights of greatness."

-- Seneca

"In civilized life, law floats in a sea of ethics."

—Earl Warren

CHAPTER ONE

PERSPECTIVE

It was November 11, 1998, at 6:30 p.m. when I got the phone call that every parent dreads. My fourteen-year-old daughter was on a cell phone in an ambulance. I could hear sirens in the background. There had been a bad accident. My daughter fought back tears as she told me that her mother had been strapped to a gurney and something was very wrong with her neck.

My wife and daughters had been forced off the highway while attempting to pass a tractor-trailer rig in the snow. While making the pass, the rig's trailer made several swings into my family's lane of traffic. As the trailer swung back and forth on the ice, it crashed into the van. With each impact, there were bright sparks as metal hit metal and breaking glass showered my wife and children. My wife's efforts to keep the vehicle on the road were not enough to overcome the black ice and slamming of the huge trailer. As my family careened into the median, the van rolled several times.

My wife's neck was broken at several levels and she sustained brain damage as a result of the accident. After two surgeries on her cervical spine and $150,000 in medical bills, she continues to battle symptoms. My children escaped from the accident with only minor cuts and bruises.

Days after the accident, it was time to weigh legal options. Having practiced law in Arizona for more than twenty years, I knew where to go for competent legal counsel. We retained a Phoenix lawyer who is one of the best trial attorneys in the state and entered a contingent fee agreement by which our attorney would be paid a third of the settlement. If the case went to trial, his fee would increase to 40% of the recovery.

After litigating for the better part of a year, our case ultimately settled a month before trial for $800,000. Out of the settlement proceeds, our attorney wrote himself a check for $280,000 after reimbursing himself for costs he'd advanced. Questions about the reasonableness of the fee have haunted me ever since.

I had no objection to paying our attorney a large fee for a job well done but was bothered that the distinction between a large fee and an excessive fee seemed blurred. My wife had been to Hell and back with accident-related pain and will live with debilitating symptoms for the rest of her life. Our attorney was in and out of our lives so quickly but walked away with a substantial share of the recovery.

Very large contingent fees have been rationalized on that basis that an attorney has undertaken some measure of risk in representing a client with no guarantee that there will ever be a recovery. This justification is not so persuasive when, from the first meeting, the attorney knows he has a client with severe injuries, liability is clear and there won't be any collection problems. If someone's sustained a severely broken neck after being rear-ended by a Greyhound bus, the question is not whether there will be a recovery. The only question is how large will it be? In those cases when there exists genuine risk for the attorney, the contingent fee agreement typically gives counsel the unfettered right to withdraw at any time.

Unbeknownst to most everyone who has ever signed a contingent fee agreement is an implied provision in it that the fee be reasonable. It's implied by the law and ethics rules which govern attorneys. The restriction limiting fees to what's reasonable is to protect the inexperienced and unsophisticated purchasers of legal services. Along these lines are ethical constraints upon attorneys to reduce their fees to what's reasonable when literal enforcement of the fee agreement would result in payment of an excessive fee. If one third of the recovery would result in an excessive fee, it should be discounted to what's reasonable.

In my wife's case, it could be argued that $50,000 to $100,000, not $280,000, would have been a reasonable fee under the circumstances. If our case had settled for $3,000,000, would our attorney claim that $1,000,000 was reasonable compensation? It needs to be kept in mind that the case did not go to trial.

More often than not, clients are unaware of ethical constraints on attorneys limiting fees to what's reasonable. When a client signs a fee agreement, all he or she knows is what's written in the document. As far as the client is concerned, whatever the outcome and whatever the demands on the attorney (or absence of demands), the specified percentage of the recovery will be allocated for the fee when there's a recovery.

Whether an attorney reduces the fee depends on the attorney's conscience and perception of his or her ethical obligation to keep the fee reasonable. When the client has no awareness of the ethical rules that govern lawyers, he is at an obvious disadvantage. Too many clients come away from the claims process not knowing whether they've been served or abused by their attorney. There's no way to document the amount of excessive fees paid to lawyers as a result of these considerations.

A few years ago, I wrote about many of these concerns in a publication sponsored by the State Bar of Arizona. A copy of the article, having to do with the attorney's ethical duty to reduce his or her contingent fee, is reproduced in the Appendix. I had hoped that writing about the problems of the system would generate constructive debate and discussion. Dialogue just might lead to action and reform.

Another obstacle to justice in the claims process is the insurance industry. More often than not, the interests of the insured are represented by well-trained and experienced adjusters whose objective is to settle as early and inexpensively as possible. Every time an insurance company settles a claim with someone who is not represented by counsel, the compensation paid is probably inadequate. "Inadequate" may mean that the claimant was shorted a few hundred dollars. It could also mean that the insurance company underpaid by several thousand dollars. The insurance industry settles millions of cases every year in which the adjuster has the advantage. As a result, the already wealthy insurance companies get wealthier because they retain hundreds of millions of dollars that belong to folks who earned them by enduring legitimate injuries.

It's unlikely that the insurance industry will ever campaign to educate the public about how to be treated fairly in the claims process. Payment of reasonable settlements would cut insurance profits. Neither is the legal profession likely to promote methods of dispute resolution that would reduce attorney involvement in auto claims. The prospects that the legal profession will ever voluntarily educate the public about ethical rules which are supposed to limit attorney's fees to what's reasonable are slim to none.

This book will fill some of the vacuum created by the competing interests of the insurance industry and legal profession. It will guide you through the claims process, minimize the involvement of attorneys in cases where they are not needed, and help you discern when legal representation is necessary. This information will put you on a level playing field with the claims adjuster in negotiating a settlement. If an attorney is to be involved, you will be better equipped to work cooperatively with the attorney and negotiate a fee agreement that is fair to both sides.

This book is about redistributing money held by insurance companies to settle auto claims. The objective is to put a greater share of a larger recovery into your pockets. The redistribution of wealth is accomplished in three ways. First, understanding basic principles of liability, damages, and the claims process will help you provide the insurance adjuster with the information he or she needs to justify payment of a larger settlement. Second, eliminating payment of the attorney's contingent fee can save 30% to 40% of the recovery. Instead, you'll seek legal counsel in a limited strategic fashion, paying by the hour, if at all, as you go. Third, you can save even more of the recovery for yourself by reducing medical bills and other obligations which often need to be paid from the settlement proceeds.

The proposed reallocation of wealth is illustrated by the pie chart on the next page. The first pie depicts a smaller settlement. Without an understanding of the claims process or an attorney, you don't know what you're entitled to or how to deal with the adjuster. Most of the settlement is allocated to repair the automobile and pay medical bills. The second pie depicts what often happens when an attorney is involved. The settlement may be larger but much of the gain is eaten up by the attorney's contingent fee. The third pie represents how the settlement proceeds can be allocated if there are no substantial attorney's fees and the medical bills and other obligations payable from the recovery are discounted.

The Settlement Pie

Without An Attorney
& Without Understanding The Claims Process

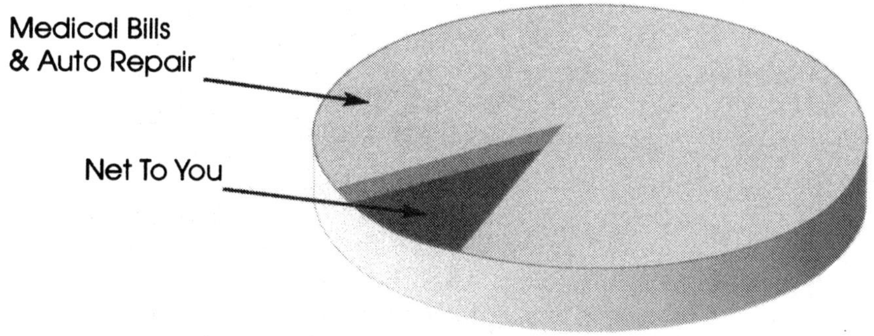

With An Attorney:
5%-20% Larger Settlement, But...

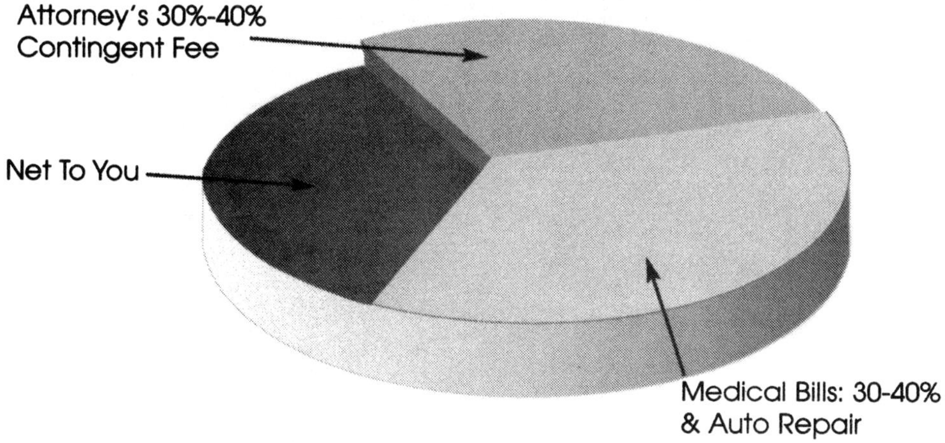

Without An Attorney
& With An Understanding of The Claims Process

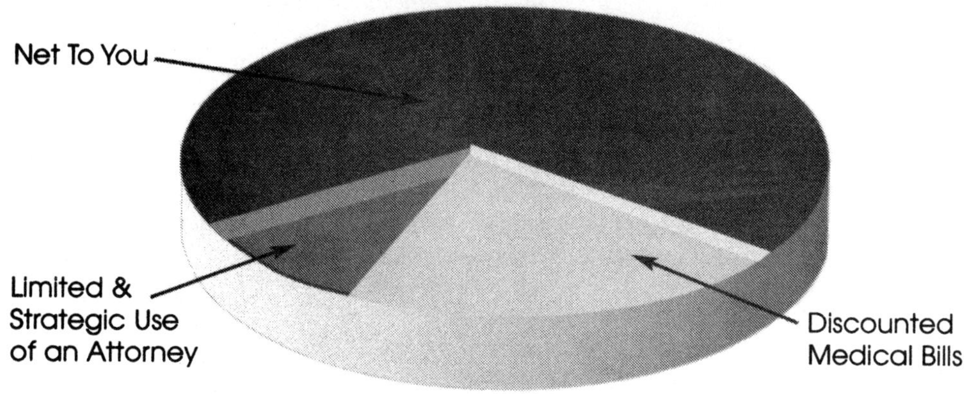

"Success in life comes not from holding a good hand, but in playing a poor hand well."

– Denis Waitley

"To be prepared is half the victory."

—Miguel Cervantes

CHAPTER TWO

CLAIMS INVESTIGATION

Take the following seven important steps in investigating your accident:

1. If the accident was investigated by a law enforcement agency, get a copy of the accident report. Generally, the law enforcement agency of the jurisdiction where the accident occurred will have investigated the accident and prepared a report. Where there is a question concerning whom to contact for the accident report, it may be necessary to confirm the precise location of the accident to determine if it occurred inside or outside the boundaries of a particular municipality or county.

   Any extra effort put forth to obtain the accident report will be worth the trouble. Accident records are full of useful information and leads. The formats for accident reports vary from state to state but contain similar detailed information. A sample report is included in the Appendix.

   For each vehicle involved in the accident, the report will include the name, date of birth, telephone number and address of each driver along with information concerning each driver's license and any restrictions to it. Details concerning the vehicles, including make, model, vehicle identification number, body style and license plate number, are generally included. Identification of the owner of the vehicle, who may be someone other than the driver, and the name, address, telephone number and other relevant data concerning the owner's insurance carrier are also contained in the report. The posted speed limit at the scene of the accident and an estimate of the speed of each vehicle just before impact are provided. Useful information is also set forth concerning the passengers including seating position, whether a safety device was used and whether any passengers were injured. Other details concerning witnesses, road and weather conditions and vehicle conditions are also disclosed.

   If citations were issued to any of the drivers, the specific alleged violations are set forth. The investigating officer's opinions with regard to who was at fault for the accident are provided along with a diagram of the accident and a narrative report by the officer that describe the accident.

2. Take photographs of the damage to the vehicle. Take plenty of photographs. Sophisticated camera equipment is not necessary. Neither are the services of a professional photographer. Safeguard the negatives. Plan to share several of the more dramatic photographs with the insurance company when settling the property damage claim.

   Do not rule out the possibility that there is damage to the vehicle which is not apparent to the naked eye. Have a mechanic inspect the undercarriage of the vehicle for damage to the frame that may not be observable in a photograph. Check out the mechanical functions of the car so that, after it has been repaired, it is operating as it was prior to the accident. Have your mechanic take notes for future reference and to assure clear communications. As we shall see, the cost of repair is a recoverable element of damages. Do everything within reason to assure the complete and professional repair of the automobile to the condition it was in prior to the accident.

3. Photograph any visible evidence of injuries. Expensive camera equipment and a professional photographer are not necessary but color film is recommended. Place a ruler along the injury in the photograph to document the length of any contusions or abrasions. Have at least one photograph of the injured party holding the front page of a newspaper to avoid any question concerning when the photograph was taken.

4. Photograph the scene of the accident. Try to capture skid marks, gauge marks in the asphalt, signs, objects which may have obscured the vision of a motorist and any other physical evidence which could be relevant to the accident.

5. Investigate the identity of any witnesses.

6. Obtain statements from all occurrence witnesses assuming what they have to say supports your claim. Most good private investigators are trained to take statements. It is possible to have the facts presented in a statement in a light most favorable to your claim.

7. If the party who caused the accident received a traffic complaint, track the course of any court proceedings involving the citation. If liability is clear, usually the responsible party will simply pay the fine and plead guilty or otherwise accept responsibility for the violation. Get evidence concerning the disposition of the traffic complaint from the court where the case was disposed of. If the cited party should challenge the traffic complaint, plan to attend the hearing and find out what is said under oath. If the other party comes to court with witnesses or other evidence, it is helpful to know in advance what you are up against. Most traffic courts electronically record the proceedings. Such recordings are public record and available to you

as a part of your investigation of the circumstances surrounding the accident. Sometimes the electronic recording is flawed. To avoid missing out on valuable evidence which may be presented at the traffic hearing, bring a court reporter. There is no reason why the judge would not allow a reporter into the court room for the purpose of making a clear record of all that goes on.

Statutes of Limitation

For every incident which gives rise to a legal claim, including auto accidents, there is a statute of limitations. This is the time frame within which a lawsuit must be filed. If a claim is not preserved by the filing of a lawsuit, it is forever lost. Statutes of limitation vary from state to state. The statutes of limitation for each state are set forth in the Appendix.

Laws, including statutes of limitation, frequently change. If the insurance lobby has anything to say about it, the statutes of limitation for personal injury claims will be shortened, not extended. Check with an attorney to confirm the statute of limitation for personal injury claims in your state. The specific statute which sets forth the pertinent limitation period is indicated in the Appendix. If there has been a change in the law, it is most likely set forth in the pocket parts to the statutes.

Another word of caution as you navigate what can seem like a mine-field in the claims process: claims against the government require a formal written demand within a relatively short time frame after the accident. Claims against the government include accidents caused by its employees. For instance, if you are rear-ended by a public school bus, you have a claim against the state and would need to comply with that state's *claims statute.*

Most municipalities, counties, and states have adopted *claims statutes.* The federal government's claims statute is the Federal Tort Claims Act.[1] To preserve the right to assert your claim and sue, if necessary, you must serve a letter on someone in a position of authority with the government which sets forth the basis of the government's liability and your damages. Failure to comply with the claims statute means you'll lose your right to sue if you don't settle.

The time frame within which the claim must be made varies from governmental entity to governmental entity. Some claims statutes require that a specific sum be included in the demand that will settle the claim. The requirements of each claims statute are different and should be carefully investigated. The public policy behind claims statutes is to afford the government an opportunity to settle and thus avoid litigation. If you have a claim against the government, get guidance from an attorney to understand not only the requirements of the relevant claims statute, but also the statute of limitation for any lawsuit which may be necessary if your claim doesn't settle.

* * *

Knowing that you have one or more years after the accident to resolve your claim, take as much time as you need to get treated. There is no reason to settle early if there is any question about your health, accident-related symptoms, or other damages. **Any attempt by the insurance adjuster to settle your claim prematurely should be politely but firmly declined.** If a claim is settled prematurely, there is no opportunity for additional reimbursement for accident-related medical expenses and other damages sustained **after** the release is signed.

To properly investigate your claim, give yourself the benefit of adequate time to get the job done right. Take however much time is available under the statute of limitations to understand the principles outlined in this manual as they relate to your claim. Patience and thorough preparation are the keys to a positive result.

"Liberty means responsibility.
That is why most men dread it."

--Man and Superman (1903)

CHAPTER THREE

LIABILITY

To settle for any amount, there must be evidence that someone was *liable* for your damages. A consideration of liability raises the question: who, if anyone, must pay? Liability has to do with negligence and fault. *Negligence* is the failure to use reasonable care. It is the failure to act as a reasonably careful person would act under the circumstances.[2] *Fault* is negligence that causes damages.[3]

If the other person's negligence was the only cause of the accident, that person is completely at fault and must pay 100% of the damages. More than one person may be at fault. The other person may claim that you were at fault or partly at fault. The other person may claim that some third party was at fault or that you **and** some third party were at fault. In determining who pays for your damages, fault must be apportioned between or among the persons whose negligence caused the accident.

In most states, you may be partly at fault for the accident and nonetheless recover damages. However, your recovery will be reduced in an amount that reflects your comparative fault. Some illustrations may be helpful:

1. **No comparative fault**. Mary is stopped at a red light in traffic. John is closing in on Mary from the rear but gets distracted by a brightly colored hot air balloon. John rear-ends Mary causing property damage to the rear of her vehicle and personal injuries. The reasonable value of Mary's damages is $10,000. John or his insurance carrier must pay the full $10,000.
2. **Comparative fault of claimant, Mary**. Mary is slowing in traffic as she approaches an intersection with four way stop signs. In violation of her state's motor vehicle laws, Mary's brake lights are in disrepair and not functioning. John closes in on Mary from the rear. John is distracted by the hot air balloon and not paying attention to the road in front of him. As

in the preceding example, the rear-end impact results in damages to Mary of $10,000. John argues that Mary was partly at fault because her brake lights were not functioning properly. He claims that, if Mary's brake lights had gone on, he would have been able to avoid the accident. In negotiating a settlement, Mary accepts 20% of the fault for the accident. John is determined to be 80% at fault. John or his insurance carrier are responsible for 80% of Mary's damages or $8,000.

3. **Comparative fault of claimant, Mary, and third party**. As in example #2, Mary is slowing in traffic as she approaches an intersection with stop signs. Mary's brake lights are not functioning. In violation of local jay-walking statutes, Zeke runs across the street in front of Mary causing her to slam on her brakes. Mary just misses Zeke but is rear-ended by John. Mary asserts a claim against John alleging that he was at fault for the accident. John contends that Mary was partly at fault because her brake lights were in disrepair. He also claims that Zeke was partly at fault because he ran across the street in front of Mary in violation of the local jay-walking statutes. Mary's total damages are $10,000. In Mary's claim against John, fault must be apportioned among John, Mary and Zeke. The allocation of fault may end up as follows:

John 50%
Mary 20%
Zeke 30%

Assuming allocation of fault with these percentages, John is responsible for 50% of Mary's $10,000 in damages, or $5,000. Mary would also have a claim against Zeke for his negligence. Zeke would pay 30% of Mary's damages or $3,000.

Apportionment of fault among parties responsible for an accident is not a precise science. Mary could argue that her failure to have properly functioning brake lights did not contribute to the accident or that, if it did, she was only 10% at fault. Mary might also claim that Zeke was more than 30% at fault. Mary could argue that if Zeke hadn't run in front of her, it's unlikely that there would have been any accident at all.

Historically, any fault or *contributory negligence* on the part of a claimant was an absolute defense, barring any recovery. It didn't matter that the claimant's negligence was only slight and that the other party's negligence was comparatively large. Six states continue to follow this restricted rule which sometimes leads to seemingly harsh results: Alabama, District of Columbia, Maryland, North Carolina, South Dakota and Virginia. In these states, it can be difficult to recover if the adjuster has evidence that your negligence, however slight, contributed to the accident.

The modern trend is to apportion fault between or among the parties. In a number of states, you're entitled to compensation if the other person was only slightly at fault and you were primarily at fault. Under this rule, if your damages were $10,000 and you were 90% at fault, you would nonetheless be entitled to recover the 10% of your damages attributable to the other party's fault, or $1,000. The 13 states which follow this rule are Alaska, Arizona, California, Florida, Kentucky, Louisiana, Michigan, Mississippi, Missouri, New Mexico, New York, Rhode Island and Washington.

In 32 states, a rule has been adopted by which a recovery is barred if you were more than 50% at fault. If you were less than 50% at fault, you're entitled to recover but your damages will be reduced according to your comparative fault. This rule has been adopted in the following 32 states: Arkansas, Colorado, Connecticut, Delaware, Georgia, Hawaii, Idaho, Illinois, Indiana, Iowa, Kansas, Maine, Massachusetts, Minnesota, Montana, Nebraska, Nevada, New Hampshire, New Jersey, North Dakota, Ohio, Oklahoma, Oregon, Pennsylvania, South Carolina, Tennessee, Texas, Utah, Vermont, West Virginia, Wisconsin, and Wyoming. Whether you were 50% at fault and the percentage of your comparative fault would be a subject of negotiation with the insurance adjuster.

When an auto claim involves an allocation of fault because liability is shared, the relative degrees of fault of the parties are likely to be a subject of negotiation with the insurance adjuster. There should be room for compromise in the settlement process concerning both the amount of damages and the amount of fault to be allocated to the insured driver with whom you are negotiating. If the case doesn't settle, a judge or jury would ultimately determine the damages and the percentages of fault.

Accidents Occurring on the Job

If you are "on the job", that means you are an employee or agent of another person or entity acting within the scope of employment when the accident occurs. The rules discussed in this section generally do not apply if you or the other party are on personal business even if driving a vehicle owned by the employer.

If you are on the Job. If you are on the job when involved in an auto accident, you should be covered by workers' compensation. Workers' compensation is an insurance system which provides security to injured workers to meet minimal needs during a period of disability. A workers' compensation claim differs from claims in conventional damages suits in two important respects. First, fault on the part of the employer and employee is eliminated. To recover benefits, the injured employee need only show that he or she was injured while on the job. Second, benefits are paid according to a definite schedule based on the type of injury sustained by the worker. The compensation to which the worker is entitled is not as much as he or she would receive in a traditional damages lawsuit but it's easier to get because there's no need to show that anyone was at fault for the accident. Each state has adopted workers' compensation statutes which entitle employees injured on the job to receive compensation until they are able to return to work.

If someone other than the employer was at fault for the accident (a *"third party"*), you would be entitled to assert a negligence claim against that party for damages. The fact that you received workers' compensation benefits does not impact the amount of damages to which you are entitled from the third party or his insurance carrier. However, upon settlement of the *third party claim*, the workers' compensation benefits must be repaid. The workers' compensation carrier is said to have a "lien" against the recovery in your claim against the third party. Insurance companies which pay workers' compensation benefits are generally willing to discount their claims against the recovery, sometimes by as much as 50%. In settling the third party claim, don't neglect to negotiate a discount of the workers' compensation lien. It can save you thousands of dollars.

If the Other Person is on the Job. In investigating the accident, find out whether the other person was on the job. If the accident report reflects that the driver was operating a vehicle owned by someone else, this could mean that he or she was on the job when the accident occurred.

The other person may have been using his or her own automobile while on a job for someone else. If the accident was caused by such an individual, there may be more than one liability insurance policy available to pay your claim: the driver's personal policy and that of the driver's employer.

If the other person was at fault for the accident while on the job for someone else, his or her negligence is imputed to the employer. The employer is *vicariously liable* for the conduct of the employee who caused the accident. From a liability standpoint, it's as if the employer caused the accident. In investigating relevant insurance coverage, it would be helpful to know that the other driver was working for a large corporation or other entity with adequate coverage or the financial ability to pay your claim.

"The things which hurt, instruct."

—Benjamin Franklin

CHAPTER FOUR

DAMAGES

Any settlement proposal to the insurance adjuster should include a discussion of both liability and damages. Understanding the compensable elements of your damages is key. Insurance companies will settle for the cost of medical care if they can get away with it. They will also try to settle before treatment is completed. Don't settle prematurely for less than what's fair compensation.

If the other party is at fault, the focus of the settlement proposal should be on damages. Not every element of damages is applicable to every claim. Some states preclude recovery for non-economic losses unless the injured party has suffered a serious impairment of body function or permanent, serious, disfigurement. The following elements of damages should be covered, if applicable:

1. <u>The nature, extent and duration of the injury</u>. This element of damages can be demonstrated by providing the insurance adjuster with copies of all relevant medical records. In earning the contingent fee which would otherwise be paid to an attorney, obtain copies of all medical records. It is helpful to have the primary treating physician prepare a brief report To Whom it May Concern describing the nature and extent of the injury along with the course of treatment and prognosis. Any report should also include a sentence which states specifically and clearly that the injury was caused by the accident. Most physicians will cooperate in the preparation of a report for a fee. The Appendix contains a sample letter for the request of medical records, bills, and a narrative report from the primary treating physician. It also includes an Authorization for Release of Medical Records form.
2. <u>Pain, discomfort, suffering, disability, disfigurement, and anxiety</u>. During recovery, keep a diary which reflects how accident-related symptoms have

impacted the quality of your life. Pain, discomfort, suffering, and anxiety are legitimate components of your damages for which you are entitled to compensation. Pain may include headaches or stiffness in the neck. Discomfort may involve going for weeks without a good night's sleep. Accident-related symptoms may prevent you from participating in a favorite sport or recreational activity. Documenting these elements of damages will provide useful ammunition in assembling a settlement package for the insurance company.

3. Reasonable expenses of necessary medical care and treatment. Accident-related medical bills are compensable if the charges were both necessary and reasonable. Recoverable medical bills include charges for ambulance service, emergency room treatment, X-rays, the reading of X-rays, prescriptions, physical therapy, medical consultations and treatment and a host of other products or services which relate to the diagnosis and treatment of your injuries. Include in your settlement package all *itemized* medical bills. The insurance adjuster will want to know from examining the bills what each charge was for. If there is a reasonable prospect that accident-related medical bills will be incurred **after** settlement of the claim, an estimate of such charges should be stated by the treating physician.
4. Lost earnings. A major aspect of your claim may be loss of income or potential income. Obtain documentation from your employer which shows your rate of pay along with copies of your W-2 forms and income tax returns for recent years. Get documentation from your employer which reflects the exact days you missed work because of the accident and the amount of money you would have earned. If the injury has prevented you from being advanced in your employment or has prevented you from obtaining employment, provide the names, addresses and telephone numbers of the witnesses who can prove this. Document in detail what services you have been prevented from performing around the house, such as supervision of the children, cleaning, maintenance, meal preparation and clean up, laundry cleaning and so forth.
5. Lost pleasures of the marital relationship. Spouses have a legal right to the company, affection, love, and services of the other spouse. This aspect of damages is commonly referred to as "loss of consortium." During convalescence, a recovering spouse is likely to be incapacitated to some degree. Household chores or cooking may not get done for lack of energy or accident-related pain and discomfort. Anxiety and irritability associated with a loss of sleep and the recovery process may result in an absence of sexual activity. You're entitled to be compensated for this intrusion upon the marital relationship and its mutual benefits.

6. Reasonable value of nursing care or services rendered gratuitously by a friend or relative. Many courts allow recovery for the reasonable value of nursing care or other services rendered gratuitously by friends or relatives.[4] The rationale is that someone receiving these services is actually detrimented because of the well-known fact that persons wear out their "welcome" with friends and relatives unless favors are returned.

   If you have had to rely on a neighbor for transportation to the doctor's office during several months of treatment, the reasonable value of such chauffeur services is compensable. In receiving such favors comes a moral obligation to repay them. Such obligation is a detriment which some courts have found to be legally compensable.

   Document nursing care and other services rendered gratuitously by family members or friends. The dates on which such services were rendered, the nature of the services and the time it took to render them should be detailed. In presenting the claim for settlement, evidence should be offered to demonstrate the commercial value of such services.

7. Property damage. In automobile accident cases, the cost of repair of the vehicle is a recoverable element of damages. Two or three repair estimates from reputable body shops will demonstrate such cost. If the repair cost exceeds the value of the automobile, the value of the vehicle on the date of the accident is the measure of damages. The best evidence of such value can be found in the classified ads of publications in which used vehicles are sold. Locate ads for the sale of similar vehicles (make, model, condition, mileage, age, etc.).

   In addition to compensation for the cost of replacement or repairs, reimbursement for lost use of the vehicle and diminution in value is also appropriate. If the automobile has been in the repair shop for two weeks, there is a reasonable prospect that car rental costs have been incurred during that time frame. Such costs are an appropriate element of damages. Even if you have not incurred out-of-pocket costs for the rental of a car, the reasonable value of substitute transportation is nonetheless compensable. If you have had to impose on friends or family for transportation, you're entitled to recover the reasonable value of such chauffeur services.

   Even if the vehicle has been properly repaired, its value may have been diminished because it was in an accident. The more serious the damage, the greater the diminution in value is likely to be. Evidence of this element of damages can be documented in an affidavit or letter by someone with expertise in automobile sales who has examined the vehicle and understands the scope of the damage and the extent of the repairs.

Journaling

Take a normal day, from when you get up in the morning until you go to bed, and detail how accident-related symptoms have changed your life. For example, the way you put on your clothes, get in and out of bed and take a bath may be impacted by the pain of your injury. Consider your life at work, play and home. Have you limited or suspended your involvement in certain hobbies or recreational activities? Has your role as a father, mother, husband, wife or parent been impacted in any way? Has your disposition changed? Has your injury affected your marital relations?

Document your pain, both at the scene of the occurrence and thereafter. Start at your head, neck, and shoulders then move down through all parts of your body. Explain in detail any problems that you have with each part of your body. Give details with regard to the medications you are taking, what they are for and whether they have any adverse side effects.

Avoid use of the words, "I can't." "Can't" suggests physical impossibility. For example, you can't use your left hand if you haven't got one. Don't say "I can't do it," "I don't do it" or "I never do it." Express your limitations with words such as "I'm not able to do it as well," "I'm not able to do it without pain" or other expressions which convey the idea that "I'm trying and I will continue to try to do more things." Everyone, including the claims adjuster, will admire you more and be more sympathetic if you try.

Contact your friends, neighbors and work associates who knew you before and after the accident. Provide their names, addresses and phone numbers. Have each witness describe on a separate sheet of paper what he or she knows about how this injury has changed your life. For example, your neighbor might indicate that you are not able to work as much around the house. Your friends might observe that you haven't bowled after the accident or engaged in other hobbies and recreational activities. It is better if these witnesses are not your relatives. It's okay to use friends because friends are more likely to have observed you.

Any discussion concerning pain should touch on the following parameters: frequency, severity, duration, circumstances that intensify pain, circumstances that lessen pain, medication taken to alleviate pain, parts of the body where pain is experienced, and other symptoms that may be associated with the pain (i.e., irritability, nausea, headache, inability to move body parts, insomnia, etc.) In the Appendix is a *Loss of Function Assessment* form which will be useful in detailing how accident-related symptoms have resulted in a loss of lifestyle with respect to a number of routine daily activities.

Future accident-related losses are compensable. If any of the components of damages discussed in this chapter are likely to continue into the future, or permanently, such anticipated losses are a proper element of damages. Evidence that pain will continue on a long-term or permanent basis or that accident-related medical bills will accrue in the future would need to be established through a physician. Long-term or permanent injuries suggest that legal counsel is necessary and appropriate. You only have one opportunity to settle for past, present, and future accident-related losses.

Preexisting Conditions

An accident may aggravate symptoms which you had experienced prior to the accident. For instance, someone who has suffered a whiplash injury may have a history of prior treatment of the neck and back. Obviously, the responsible party is not liable for symptoms and injuries which preceded the accident. However, if preexisting injuries were aggravated or made worse by the accident, you are entitled to full and fair compensation for the aggravation.

A preexisting health problem may have rendered the victim of an accident more susceptible to injury. Such an individual is nonetheless entitled to full and fair compensation for accident-related injuries even if a normally healthy person would not have suffered a similar injury.

If you have a preexisting condition or are unusually susceptible to injury, these issues should be addressed with the adjuster. Since the insurance company's attorney would be entitled to discover your health history in any event in litigation, relevant pre-accident medical records should be obtained and disclosed. Your treating physician could explain in a report how the accident aggravated your preexisting symptoms or why you were more susceptible to injury because of the previous health problem.

"Even if you're on the right track,
you'll get run over if you just sit there."

– Will Rogers

"To appreciate heaven well, 'tis good for
a man to have some fifteen minutes of hell."

—Will Carleton

CHAPTER FIVE

WHIPLASH

Perhaps the most common auto accident is the rear-end collision. An injury which often results to the occupants of the rear-ended vehicle is a neck injury known as "whiplash."

Whiplash injuries raise unique challenges in asserting a claim. Often the vehicle which was rear-ended does not sustain dramatic damage. Sometimes the damage is barely noticeable. It should follow, according the claims adjuster that, in the absence of significant damage to the automobile, there can be no real injury to its occupants.

Symptoms of whiplash generally do not include the external shedding of blood or broken bones. It's unlikely that evidence of the injury would appear on x-ray. In the absence of objective evidence that there's been an injury, fraud and malingering are sometimes suspected by the claims adjuster. Whiplash injuries are often treated with positive results by chiropractors. Sometimes chiropractors are accused of unnecessary treatment and excessive charges. Notwithstanding these considerations which may surface in asserting a claim for whiplash, the injury is real and the symptoms can be debilitating.

Understanding the dynamics of the injury will help you overcome claims by the adjuster that "it was only a light impact." A basic law of physics involved in a rear-end collision is inertia. Inertia means that objects which are standing still tend to remain still and objects set in motion tend to continue in motion. In a rear-end collision, the head, which weighs 16 to 20 pounds, is an object which tends to stand still because it is unsupported and not in contact with any other objects in the car. When the car is struck from the rear and suddenly propelled forward, the body and shoulders are, in essence, driven out from under the head. The head stays still while the shoulders and trunk are pushed out from under it. Thus, you have one portion of the body being set in motion and another portion of the body, the head, which remains still. When this occurs, the head snaps backward, severely stressing the neck. The snapping of the head in a backward direction is called *extension*, or *hyperextension*. Often, the head will recoil so far back that it will actually strike the back window of a truck or car.

After the hyperextension phase as the car abruptly stops, either because it has rear-ended another car or the driver is applying the brakes, the head recoils forward because of the momentum of the stopping car. This forward movement of the head, after it reaches its full hyperextension backward, is called *flexion*, or *hyperflexion*. *Hyper*, in medical parlance, means excessive. This is why physicians sometimes call these injuries hyperextension-flexion injuries.

The neck is more subject to injury than any other portion of the vertebral column. It is vulnerably placed between the dorsal spine, which is relatively immobile, and the skull, a weight which must be balanced on the cervical spine and held in place by the supporting capsular, ligamentous, cartilaginous, and muscular structure.[5]

During the initial neck extension phase, the anterior ligaments on the cervical spine are stressed. If the stress is sufficiently great, the ligaments may tear or rupture. The delayed flexion will stress and sometimes tear the posterior structures. This leads to bruising and internal bleeding.[6] The effects of the flexion may be enhanced if the occupant is wearing a seat belt with shoulder harness.

Some whiplash injuries are relatively benign with symptoms that resolve in a few weeks or a month. Others can result in severe, debilitating, and chronic health problems. Understanding the dynamics which impact the severity of the extension-flexion injury can be useful in explaining why your symptoms may persist and cause continuing pain, discomfort and loss of lifestyle. Some of the more significant considerations include the following:

1. *Head rotation.* If your head is rotated at the moment of impact, the injury is likely to be more severe. When the head is rotated, the cervical spine tends to be more rigid, less resilient and more susceptible to injury. If you're engaged in conversation with a passenger and having eye contact with that passenger at the moment of impact, your head will be rotated in the direction of the occupant with whom you are conversing. You may be reaching for something in the glove box and looking in that direction to open or close the box at the moment of impact. In a more dangerous scenario, you may turn completely around to look through the rear window upon hearing the screech of tires from the vehicle that's closing in from the rear. In that situation, your upper torso and cervical spine may be fully rotated at the moment of impact. See, for example, the Demand Letter in the Appendix at page 109 in which it is pointed out to the adjuster that the claimant was fully rotated, upon impact, because he had turned around to

look back upon hearing the screech of tires. As a general proposition, the greater the head rotation, the greater the prospects of more serious injury.

2. *Awareness of impending impact.* A lack of awareness that there's about to be a collision means there's no opportunity to brace for the impact. An opportunity to tighten the muscles around the cervical spine would reduce the prospects of hyper-extension and hyper-flexion and the resulting strains, sprains and tearing of the ligaments which support the neck and head.

3. *Seat belt use.* Although seat belts save lives, the shoulder harness tends to contribute to more serious whiplash injuries. A secure harness holds the upper torso firmly in place. This results in greater loading on the cervical spine as the head is rapidly thrust forward.

4. *Force of the impact.* A rear-end impact from a vehicle traveling 50 miles per hour is likely to cause more injury than the impact from a gentle nudge of a vehicle that's moving very slowly. This is not to say, however, that genuine whiplash injuries are not caused at lower crash speeds. **"Large epidemiological studies have shown that nearly 80% of whiplash injuries occur at crash speeds below 12 mph. Other studies have shown that the threshold of damages for many passenger cars ranges from 8.5 mph to over 12 mph. Clearly then, a large percentage of real injuries occur in the absence of significant vehicle damage."** [7]

5. *Gender.* Females tend to be injured more frequently and severely than males.[8]

6. *Age of the occupant.* Tolerance to impact decreases over age 40. Injury to occupants over 65 results in a substantially poorer prognosis. "For the elderly, neck injury can be very serious. The degenerative spine is biomechanically 'stiffer', behaving more like a single long bone than like a set of articulating structures. Deforming forces are less evenly dissipated and more damage is done." [9]

In any whiplash case, there's a likelihood that one or more of these dynamics will be a consideration in explaining the nature and extent of the injury. For instance, it's the law of the land that you wear a seatbelt. If a firm shoulder harness held your upper torso in place and this contributed to a more serious neck injury, this consideration should be pointed out to the adjuster. It's equally possible that you were unaware of the impending impact or your head was rotated in some manner when you were hit. Dialogue with your treating physician about these dynamics may be helpful. The doctor could refer to these considerations in any report that's prepared in connection with the settlement process.

Symptoms of whiplash include neck ache, neck stiffness with limited movement, headache, shoulder pain, neck tenderness, spasm, dizziness, fatigue, memory impairment, anxiety, irritability, tinnitus, and weakness. Journaling, to document these symptoms and the corresponding loss of lifestyle, is an important discipline.

If serious symptoms persist without improvement over an extended period of time, get treated by someone other than or in addition to a chiropractor or physical therapist. The objective would be to rule out damage to the spine itself such as a damaged ["herniated"] disc or fracture. An examination by a neurosurgeon may be indicated to explore these diagnoses. Sophisticated x-ray equipment is available to take pictures of the spine for these purposes. If more serious problems are diagnosed, the prospect of spinal surgery may become a reality.

"To get to the promised land you have to negotiate your way through the wilderness."

—Author Unknown

CHAPTER SIX

INSURANCE

A common concern for many who have been involved in auto accidents is payment for treatment necessitated by accident-related injuries. Consider the most common forms of insurance available to meet this obligation:

1. *Medical payment benefits.* Your own auto insurance policy may include medical payment benefits coverage ["med pay"] to pay medical bills necessitated by an auto accident. Such coverage is available to the driver and passengers, up to the limits specified in the policy, without regard to who was at fault. In some states it's not necessary to reimburse the insurance company for med pay benefits upon settlement of a liability claim against a responsible party. The cost of med pay is relatively inexpensive. One of the first sources to consider for help in paying medical bills is your own policy's med pay coverage.
2. *Health insurance.* Look to your health insurance as a source for payment of your medical bills. If you later receive compensation for your injuries from another source, you may be obligated to repay some or all of the benefits received. Whether and how much you have to repay varies with the type of health insurance. Many health plans pay no attention to whether you have received accident compensation for the same injuries that the health plan covered. Some plans, however, specify the right to reimbursement out of any damages award or settlement you receive and aggressively enforce that right.
3. *Medicare and Medicaid.* Medicare and Medicaid are federal government programs which provide medical coverage for persons over 65 [Medicare] and others with low income [Medicaid]. Both programs are entitled to reimbursement if you settle a damages claim against someone responsible for your injuries. Medicare and Medicaid administrators often don't have

any idea that you've asserted a claim for damages against a third person and usually don't bother to check.

4. *Workers' compensation.* Every state has workers' compensation laws to compensate employees who are injured on the job. If you are injured while working for an employer, whether at your place of work or away from your normal job site, workers' compensation will pay your medical bills and a portion of your lost wages. Workers' compensation is your only remedy against your employer even if the employer's negligence caused your injuries. If you file both a workers' compensation claim and a claim against a party other than your employer who was at fault for the accident, you'll need to repay the workers' compensation benefits if there's a recovery.

If there's no insurance to pay for treatment, find a physician who is willing to wait for payment until your claim settles. Many doctors are willing to take a *lien* against the recovery if there's an insured party at fault for the accident. Formalize the agreement with a *Doctor's Lien*, a sample of which is provided in the Appendix. The Doctor's Lien authorizes direct payment of the medical bill by the insurance company when your claim settles.

If there's no insurance and you're unable to find a physician willing to take a lien against the recovery, you'll need to pay out of pocket for treatment as you receive it. Even if there's an insured party who is clearly at fault for your injuries, insurance companies are generally unwilling to pay piecemeal for the cost of your treatment as it's incurred. They'll pay in a lump sum only upon final settlement.

For repair or replacement of your automobile, there are generally two options. If your own auto insurance policy includes collision [or "car damage" or "property damage"] coverage, you may have your own insurance company pay that expense, subject to any deductible. Collision coverage is available without regard to who was at fault. If your insurance company pays this expense, it will seek reimbursement from the party responsible for the accident. The other option with respect to repair or replacement of your automobile is to have the insurance company for the responsible party pay for it. A benefit to settling the property damage claim with the other party's insurance company is that there's no deductible.

With regard to benefits paid for medical expenses or property damage, determine whether the insurance company has a right to reimbursement from the party responsible for the loss. Such right is referred to as *subrogation.* Whether there's a right to reimbursement depends on the policy and the law of the state where the accident occurred. If you can receive insurance benefits without having to repay them, you'll be dollars ahead. Many insurance companies are willing to accept less than they're owed in resolving a subrogation claim. It's worth the time and effort to investigate the rights of insurers to reimbursement then negotiate a compromise of their subrogation claim. This subject is discussed in detail in Chapter Eight.

If another person is at fault or partly at fault for the accident, investigate the identity of that individual's liability insurance carrier. This information is easy to get from the accident report or the other party. With one or two calls to the insurance company, you'll be in touch with the claims department and find out who's been assigned to settle the matter. Note that person's name, address, phone number, fax number, and the claim number. This is the person with whom there will be considerable dialogue as you navigate the claims process.

The insurance company may not be willing to disclose its insured's policy limits available to resolve your claim. Preliminarily, the adjuster will confirm that your claim is covered by the policy and that it was in force on the date of the accident. The adjuster will attempt to get a statement from you concerning the facts of the accident and your injuries. The adjuster will also try to settle your claim early and inexpensively. Do not accede to the adjuster's requests for a statement. Neither should you consider an early settlement especially if the nature and extent of your injuries are unknown.

More than one person's liability policy may cover your damages. In that situation, one insurance company will provide "primary" coverage and the other will provide "secondary" or "excess" coverage. The primary coverage will pay your damages up to the policy limits. If the primary coverage is exhausted, the secondary coverage is available to pay the rest of your damages. If there's more than one liability policy available to pay your damages, submit a claim against both. The insurance companies will sort out who's primary and who's secondary.

No Fault Automobile Insurance

A number of states have adopted some form of no-fault automobile insurance law, sometimes referred to as Personal Injury Protection [PIP]. No-fault coverage eliminates injury liability claims and lawsuits when the damages are less serious. In exchange, the injured person gets reimbursed by his or her own insurance company for medical bills and lost wages, up to certain relatively modest limits, without regard to who was at fault. There is no compensation for pain, suffering, anxiety, emotional distress, and inconvenience. No-fault coverage usually does not apply to damage to the vehicle. Property damage claims are resolved by asserting a claim against the party at fault. Some form of no-fault automobile insurance law has been adopted in the following states:

Arkansas
Colorado
Delaware
District of Columbia
Florida
Hawaii
Kansas
Kentucky
Maryland
Massachusetts
Michigan
Minnesota
New Jersey
New York
North Dakota
Oregon
Pennsylvania
South Dakota
Texas
Utah
Virginia

After you file your no-fault claim against your own carrier, you may also be allowed to assert a liability claim against the responsible person to obtain compensation above and beyond what was covered by the no-fault benefits. Whether you're entitled to assert such a claim depends on the law of the no-fault state where the accident occurred.

Some states have no restriction on your right to assert a liability claim against the party who caused the accident after receiving no-fault benefits. In the following states, you can always file a liability claim against the person at fault for damages in excess of your no-fault benefits:

Arkansas
Delaware
Maryland
Oregon
Pennsylvania
South Dakota
Texas
Virginia

Other no-fault states have different types of thresholds that you must reach before you're entitled to pursue a claim for full compensation against the party at fault. Some states have a medical expense monetary threshold and some a serious injury threshold. Some states have both. States with both requirements permit a liability claim if an injured person meets either one. The following no-fault states permit a liability claim and lawsuit against the person at fault when the injured party has incurred **necessary** medical expenses over a certain limit:

Colorado	$2,500
District of Columbia	your policy's PIP benefit amount
Hawaii	your policy's PIP benefit amount
Kansas	$500
Kentucky	$1,000
Massachusetts	$500
Minnesota	$4,000

North Dakota	$2,500
Utah	$1,000

The threshold is indicated for each state. One you have reached your necessary medical expense threshold, you may assert a liability claim against the party at fault. These states also permit a liability claim or lawsuit if a serious injury threshold is met instead of the medical expense threshold.

In some no-fault states, the laws allow an injured person to assert a liability claim against the party at fault if a "serious" injury has been sustained without regard to the amount spent on medical treatment. Injuries that qualify as serious are defined by each state's law as follows:

Colorado	permanent disability or permanent disfigurement
District of Columbia	substantial permanent scarring or disfigurement, substantial permanent impairment, or substantial total impairment lasting 180 days
Florida	permanent injury or significant and permanent scarring or disfigurement
Hawaii	significant permanent loss of use of a body part or function or permanent and serious disfigurement resulting in mental or emotional distress
Kansas	permanent disfigurement, fracture of weightbearing bone or compound, comminuted, compressed or displaced fracture of any bone, permanent injury or permanent loss of a body function
Kentucky	permanent disfigurement, fracture of weightbearing bone or compound, comminuted, compressed or displaced fracture of any bone, permanent injury or permanent loss of a body function
Massachusetts	permanent and serious disfigurement, fractured bone, substantial loss of hearing or sight

Michigan	serious impairment of a body function or permanent and serious disfigurement
Minnesota	60 days disability, permanent injury, or permanent disfigurement
New Jersey	some permanent disability or full disability of over 180 days, significant disfigurement, or permanent loss of a bodily function
New York	significant disfigurement, bone fracture, permanent limitation of use of body o organ, significant limitation of body function or system, or substantially full disability for 90 days
North Dakota	serious and permanent disfigurement or disability of more than 60 days
Utah	bone fracture, permanent disability, or permanent disfigurement

Because of the somewhat vague statutory definitions of the threshold injuries and the subjective nature of many medical evaluations, it may not be clear whether your injuries meet the threshold. If so, whether your injuries qualify are likely to be among the issues for negotiation with the insurance company of the party at fault.

Uninsured and Underinsured Motorist Coverage

There are many drivers on the road without any liability insurance. If you're in an accident caused by an uninsured driver, one of the places to look for compensation is your own policy for *uninsured motorist coverage.* Such coverage is required by law in some states. Normally, property damage is not covered. Damage to your vehicle caused by an uninsured driver would be covered by the collision coverage of your own policy.

Most policies will pay for injuries sustained by you, drivers, and passengers covered by the policy up to your uninsured motorist coverage limits. The claim against your own insurance company will be processed as if it were a liability claim against another party. Subjects of negotiation with the adjuster would include the other person's liability, the extent of your comparative fault, if any, and your damages.

Many drivers purchase just enough liability insurance to meet their state's laws. Such coverage is often inadequate to reimburse an injured person for all the damages to which he or she is entitled. *Underinsured motorist coverage* allows you to collect compensation beyond what the other driver's insurance will pay up to the limits specified in your policy. You'll need to show your insurance company that the other driver was underinsured for your damages. Get a letter from the other party's insurance company that sets forth the policy limits for that person's liability coverage. Also confirm in writing settlement of your claim with the other party's carrier for an amount equal to such policy limits.

* * * * * *

In investigating insurance benefits from any source, review the relevant policies and related documents. Examine all amendments and endorsements. Each policy will have a declarations sheet which summarizes the coverage. If it's necessary to call the insurance company or your agent for copies of insurance records, do so. Don't be intimidated by fine print or legalese. If you need guidance from your agent or an attorney to make sense of the documents, take the time to get it.

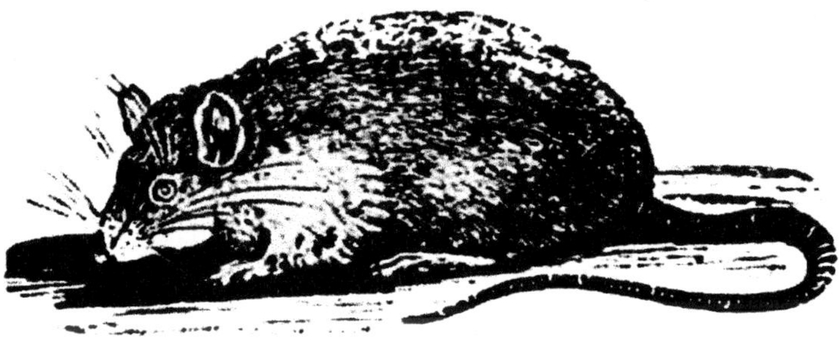

"If you can dream it, you can do it. Always remember this whole thing was started by a mouse."

– Walt Disney

"The minute you start talking about
what you are going to do if you lose, you have lost."

--George Schultz

CHAPTER SEVEN

PRESENTING THE CLAIM

Some elements of damages are objective and easy to calculate. If the charges for accident-related medical treatment were both reasonable and necessary, it's a simple matter to add them up. If you've lost time from work because of your injuries, it's just as easy to calculate the lost wages. But how do you get reasonably compensated for pain, discomfort, and anxiety?

Usually, there is a correlation between compensation awarded for pain and discomfort and dollars paid for medical care. A general rule of thumb adopted by many insurance adjusters and personal injury attorneys is that the settlement value of a claim equals two to three times the accident-related medical bills. Thus, if you've incurred $5,000 in necessary medical expenses and those charges are shown to be reasonable, you can expect to settle the claim for $10,000 to $15,000.

Another way to analyze the value of your claim is through *jury verdict research.* Most law libraries have access to this data. Locate other cases which have been resolved by settlement or trial involving injuries similar to yours. Other similar cases are evidence of the value of your claim. Jury Verdict Research (800-341-7874) maintains a nationwide database of plaintiff and defense verdicts and settlements resulting from personal injury claims. The data is reported, verified, tabulated and analyzed to determine values and trends in personal injury verdicts.

In the Appendix are several settlement proposals to insurance companies from actual claims which were settled without litigation. For most of the claims, liability was not an issue and the focus of the proposal was on damages. The letters were prepared and presented after a thorough investigation of the facts. Along with the letters, copies of accident reports, witness statements, medical records, bills, photographs, and the other fruit of the claim investigation were included.

Your settlement proposal ("demand letter") represents weeks or months of record keeping, journaling, investigation, research, and analysis concerning your claim. If your claim is to settle for a reasonable amount, it's because your letter is well-reasoned, detailed, and supported by the appropriate back up documentation.

Every settlement proposal will include a discussion of both liability or allocation of fault and damages. If liability is not at issue, your letter will simply say so. The demand will conclude with a proposal to settle for a sum certain which allows room for negotiation.

At some point before presenting the claim to the insurance company, a determination needs to be made concerning what the claim is worth. Don't ask for an amount that is substantially in excess of what's reasonable. If the objective is to settle for $15,000, don't ask for $50,000. To propose settlement for an unreasonably high figure will send a signal to the insurance adjuster that you don't know what your claim is worth or you don't know what you're doing. Making an unreasonable demand may only drive a wedge between you and the insurance company rendering compromise and settlement unlikely. Thus, if the objective is to settle the claim for $15,000, make a good faith argument in your settlement proposal that the claim is worth $20,000, perhaps $25,000. The insurance company will expect you to accept less than the figure that has been presented in the proposal.

Legal Research

One vast source of knowledge is the law library. You don't need an attorney or money to access the wealth of information contained within its thousands of volumes. You will need persistence, humility and a willingness to seek guidance from someone who knows something about legal research. Most law librarians are ready, willing and able to provide such guidance.

If, for instance, the focus of the claim is on damages, there is a wealth of useful information in the law library on those aspects of damages that are unique to your claim. Reviewing relevant case law, treatises and statutes will provide insights concerning what damages are recoverable, what they are worth and how to document them.

Law libraries have many publications in numerous forms that can be useful in researching a claim. They contain hundreds of thousands of reported cases on every conceivable subject. The prospects of finding a case with facts similar to yours are excellent.

In researching and reviewing cases, note the names and locations of the attorneys for the parties indicated in the text. If the case isn't too old, the attorneys can be located and contacted. For instance, the Appendix contains a copy of the Swartz case that involved the attorney who was disciplined for charging an excessive contingent fee. The first page of the case indicates that the State Bar was represented by Stephen L. Weiss, from Phoenix. Mr. Swartz was represented by Jack C. Cavness, also of Phoenix. If you had a question about an issue covered in the case, call Mr. Weiss or Mr. Cavness to discuss the matter.

Another way to squeeze even more information from a reported case is to inspect the court documents, known as *pleadings*, which comprise the record of the proceedings. The history of any case, from the filing of the complaint through the appellate court proceedings, is available to be copied and studied. For whatever the copy costs would be, the clerk of the court in the county and state where the case originated will provide a record of the proceedings. Another source for copies of court-related documents are the attorneys for the litigants. Many attorneys would be flattered and eager to assist someone who had taken enough of an interest in a case they had litigated through the appellate process to look them up.

Independent Medical Examinations

The other party's insurance company may ask you to submit to a physical examination by its own doctor. The insurance company may suspect over-treatment, overcharging or misdiagnosis by your physician.

During litigation, the other party has a right to have you evaluated by another physician. In the absence of a lawsuit, there is no such right. The question becomes whether to cooperate with the insurance company in its request for the evaluation. In theory, the evaluation is conducted by an **independent** physician. Because the evaluations are to be objective and undertaken by a neutral doctor, they are referred to as *"independent medical evaluations"* or IMEs.

Often, there is reason to question the independence of the physicians hired by the insurance company. Some doctors who perform "independent" medical evaluations have lucrative business relationships with the insurance company. The results of such examinations are often predictable, favoring the interests of the insured. They may conclude that you have been over-treated, misdiagnosed, or are malingering. The bias of some examining physicians can be a result of the corrupting influence of large amounts of money paid to such doctors by the insurance industry over a period of time. In more extreme cases, defense-oriented IME doctors will prostitute themselves and compromise their professional reputation and sound medical judgment to reach a conclusion they are willing to give in exchange for a fee.

Refusal to consent to the requested evaluation could jeopardize progress toward settlement. It is unlikely that there would be any significant movement toward a resolution of your claim unless and until the insurance company gets the IME it has decided is necessary.

Agreeing to the examination could be justified on the basis that the insurance company will get its IME sooner or later. Failing an out-of-court settlement, the insured would have the right to compel an IME in the context of litigation. If you have submitted to a pre-litigation IME, it is unlikely that the insurance company would be entitled to a second examination in the absence of some significant change of circumstances.

An insurance company's request for an IME is a signal that it's time for a consultation with a qualified personal injury attorney. The attorney may know something about the proposed IME doctor and whether such doctor has a bias in favor of the insurance industry. You may be surprised to learn that the proposed IME doctor is truly independent. An objective evaluation by the insurance company's physician could substantiate the legitimacy of your injuries. In that event, the prospects of settlement would be enhanced considerably. If the proposed IME doctor has a reputation for being defense-oriented and predictable, there may be room to negotiate for the use of another physician who is not burdened with that bias.

Why Settle?

This book emphasizes settlement as the objective in resolving an auto accident claim. The options to settlement are either abandonment of the claim or litigation. If liability is tenuous or there's a question whether your damages were caused by the accident, the best option may be to simply walk away from the claim.

Litigation has several disadvantages. The cost of the process may be significant. Even when working with an attorney on a contingent fee basis, there may be several thousand dollars in costs for which you would be responsible *as they are incurred.* Unless the claim is pursued in small claims court, involvement of an attorney means paying a substantial hourly rate or a contingent fee of 30% to 40% of the recovery.

Litigation is time consuming. The process can take a year or more, depending on the venue. In some large metropolitan areas, such as Los Angeles, it can take three or four years to get to trial. Along with the delay, come uncertainty and the emotional toll of the process. Finality in litigation can be elusive. A jury verdict after a trial does not necessarily signify the end of the process and a final resolution of the claim. There may be post trial proceedings and appeals which would extend the process for additional months or years. The end result of an appeal could result in another trial. The process also means an escalation of costs.

To avoid the expense and uncertainty of litigation, cases are often settled for less than they are worth. Whether to draw a line in the sand and fight, settle, or walk away can be a difficult decision. An understanding of the information gleaned from this book, legal counsel from one or more trusted attorneys, and a measure of wisdom should lead you to the right decision.

"Let us never negotiate out of fear. But never let us fear to negotiate."

--John F. Kennedy

CHAPTER EIGHT

COMPROMISING LIENS

Within the context of settlement and settlement negotiations, keep track of who's paid benefits for your health care, automobile repair, lost wages, and otherwise. Of the entities who have paid, determine who is entitled to reimbursement from the settlement. An insurer's right to reimbursement, or *subrogation rights*, if any, are set forth in the policy. If the fine print is difficult to understand, call the insurance company or the adjuster who sold you the coverage to find out whether the insurance company is entitled to reimbursement when and if there's a recovery.

Don't assume that every insurer has subrogation rights with respect to benefits paid out. An insurer's right to reimbursement depends on the policy and state law. For instance, in some states, automobile insurers are not entitled to recover medical payment benefits. Health insurance companies do not necessarily have subrogation rights. In your liability claim, the insurance company of the responsible party is probably not entitled to know that you've received benefits which do not need to be repaid from settlement.

In any case, be sensitive to who is entitled to what when the case settles. If a health care provider, insurer, or other creditor is entitled to payment, it should not be ignored when the ability to satisfy the obligation from settlement money exists.

It's common for physicians to formalize their right to recovery from the settlement by lien agreements. A lien simply gives the unpaid creditor a *security interest* in the recovery. The creditor is deemed to own, as it were, that portion of the recovery that will allow for repayment. The unpaid creditors who have rights in the recovery are collectively referred to as *"lien claimants."* A sample form of *Doctor's Lien* is included in the Appendix. Note that it authorizes the insurance adjuster to pay the doctor's bill directly from the settlement.

Compromising lien claims against the recovery can put a greater share of the settlement in your pocket. A doctor who is owed $2,000 might be willing to settle for $1,000 or $1,500. It's been said that "one in the hand is worth two in the bush." If the physician can facilitate a settlement by reducing his or her bill, the account will be satisfied and the doctor will receive something of value for services rendered.

The lien claimants understand that if your claim doesn't settle, it could be many months or years before there's a recovery to fund repayment. They also understand that, failing settlement, litigation is inevitable. The litigation process may take years. The prospects of an adverse result after litigating could mean that there would be *no fund* from which repayment could be made. Doctors, health care providers, and insurance companies are willing to settle for less than what they are owed because of these considerations.

Negotiating the compromise of liens is a process. In asking lien claimants to discount their bills, let them know the insurance company that is proposing to pay the settlement, the amount of the proposed settlement, the total medical bills, and whether other health care providers have agreed to discount their bills and, if so, by what amount. If there's an attorney involved in the process, they would want to know whether the attorney is willing to reduce his contingent fee and, if so, by what amount. The objective behind the lien compromise process is for everyone to give away a little to allow for a more equitable distribution of the settlement pie. When a deal has been struck with regard to a lien compromise, confirm it in writing.

Compromising Attorney's Liens

One of the objectives of this book is to assist you in identifying those cases which can be resolved without retaining an attorney under a contingent fee agreement. If a lawyer has been hired for a claim in which representation was thought to be necessary, this chapter will provide guidance.

The contingent fee agreement is an arrangement in which the attorney is given a lien against the recovery. The lien is often thirty percent (30%) to forty percent (40%) of the recovery. In some respects, the attorney's lien is similar to that of the other lien claimants discussed in the preceding section. In other respects, the attorney's lien is unique because attorneys are subject to certain ethical constraints which require them to keep their fees *reasonable*.

We've discussed why insurance companies and health care providers are often willing to compromise their liens. An attorney has some of the same motives for agreeing to a fee that is less than what was provided for in the contingent fee agreement: by taking a smaller share of a proposed settlement and putting more dollars into the pocket of his client, the prospects of settlement are enhanced. Any compromise which makes litigation unnecessary has benefits to all concerned.

Under some circumstances, an attorney has an ethical duty to reduce his or her lien. In an Arizona case, an attorney was suspended from the practice of law for not compromising his one-third contingent fee. A review of the facts from In the Matter of Swartz[10] will make some important points about when an attorney has a duty to reduce his or her fee.

In Swartz, the client was seriously injured when hit by a car. He sustained severe multiple injuries. One leg was eventually amputated. The client, Steven Sarge, was on the job when he was injured. Because he was working, he received workers' compensation benefits. The insurance carrier that paid the benefits had a statutory lien against the recovery in Sarge's personal injury claim arising out of the auto accident.

In Sarge's claim against the motorist, there was no question about who was at fault. The driver was covered by two separate liability policies with limits of $50,000 and $100,000. Shortly after Sarge retained Swartz on a one-third contingent fee basis, one of the liability carriers turned over its $100,000 policy limits. About two months later, the second carrier paid its $50,000 policy limits. The time demands on Swartz in negotiating payment of the liability insurance money were minimal. Of the $150,000 obtained by Swartz, he took $50,000 as his one-third contingent fee. The insurance carrier that paid the workers' compensation benefits received most of the remaining $100,000 by virtue of its lien against the recovery. Sarge got nothing.

Even though Swartz took no more than he was entitled to under the contingent fee agreement, the Arizona Supreme Court concluded that the fee was excessive and disciplined him. The Court reasoned that, in light of the clear liability of the motorist who injured Sarge, there really was no *contingency.* The Court observed that there were no difficult problems in the case. In obtaining the $150,000 in liability insurance money, there were no significant demands on Swartz' time. The Court also thought it was significant that Swartz didn't have to file a lawsuit. With regard to the one-third contingent fee, the Court observed that, although such fee agreements are often proper *when contracted,* they may turn out to be excessive. With regard to the attorney's ethical duty to reduce his contingent fee, the Court concluded:

> We hold, therefore, that if **at the conclusion of a lawyer's services,** it appears that a fee, which seemed reasonable when agreed upon, has become excessive, the attorney may not stand upon the contract; he must reduce the fee.

The principle gleaned from Swartz is that if the attorney's contingent fee turns out to be out of proportion to the time and effort invested by the attorney in the claim, a reduction of the fee should be considered. Ask the attorney for an itemization that reflects time spent providing legal services in connection with the case. Were there any onerous demands on the attorney's time because of the case? Did the claim have any unique or difficult problems? If the attorney is paid the full contingent fee, what will his hourly rate be? $500 per hour? $1,000 per hour? $2,000 per hour?

The Swartz opinion has an excellent discussion of the benefits and disadvantages of the contingent fee agreement from the attorney's and client's perspective. It focuses on the ethical duty of legal counsel to reduce his or her fee under certain circumstances. The opinion also reviews the issue of lien compromises by third party insurers such as the industrial carrier that paid Sarge's workers' compensation benefits. For these reasons, a copy of the opinion is included in the Appendix. Although the case originates in Arizona, the legal and ethical issues addressed are of general application throughout the United States. Before approaching legal counsel to request a fee reduction, a review and understanding of the Swartz opinion is encouraged.

"It's not over 'til it's over."

--Yogi Berra

CHAPTER NINE

FINAL SETTLEMENT LOGISTICS

Final settlement of the property damage claim is relatively quick and simple. When an agreement has been reached concerning what should be paid for damage to or replacement of the automobile, write a confirming letter to the adjuster. Generally, the adjuster will send you a letter and release document which you'll need to sign and return before the settlement check is processed. Be sure there's nothing in the letter or release to suggest that you're giving up claims other than for damage to or replacement of the vehicle. The same is true for the settlement check when it's received from the insurance company. If there's language on the front or back of the check by which claims, other than for property damage, are released, do not negotiate the check. For instance, if "general release" or words to that effect appear in either the letter from the adjuster, the release document or on the check, hold off on signing.

With respect to final resolution of the bodily injury claim, settlement precludes you from ever again seeking additional compensation from the other party's insurance company. This is so even if accident-related complications or symptoms should surface after settlement. The following standard "Release in Full of All Claims and Rights" makes the point that there's no coming back for additional compensation after the case is settled:

RELEASE IN FULL OF ALL CLAIMS AND RIGHTS

FOR AND IN CONSIDERATION of the sum of $10,000.00, receipt of which is hereby acknowledged, JOHN DOE and JANE DOE release, acquit, and forever discharge ABC BRANDS, INC., and XYZ STORES, INC., and their assigns, employees, employers, principals, agents, representatives, heirs, executors, officers, directors, administrators, and insurers, (hereinafter "Released Parties"), from any and all rights, claims, causes of action, actions, demands and damages of any kind, known or unknown, existing or arising in the future, resulting from or related to personal injuries, loss of income or property damage arising from an incident which occurred on or about the _____ day of December, __________, in ___________ County, Arizona. WE UNDERSTAND THAT THIS IS ALL THE MONEY OR CONSIDERATION WE WILL RECEIVE FROM THE RELEASED PARTIES AS A RESULT OF THE INCIDENT .

We understand and agree that the payment of the above mentioned sum is not to be construed as an admission of liability on the part of the Released Parties, liability for the incident being expressly denied by Released Parties, but is the compromise and settlement of a highly disputed claim.

WE ALSO UNDERSTAND THAT THIS IS A RELEASE NOT ONLY OF CLAIMS AGAINST THE RELEASED PARTIES REGARDING INJURIES NOW KNOWN, AND REGARDING ANY DAMAGES, INJURIES OR COMPLICATIONS WHICH MAY DEVELOP IN THE FUTURE FROM SAID PRESENTLY EXISTING INJURIES, BUT ALSO FOR ANY ADDITIONAL INJURIES OR COMPLICATIONS THEREOF WHICH MAY ARISE, DIRECTLY OR INDIRECTLY, FROM THE AFOREMENTIONED INCIDENT, WHETHER RELATED OR UNRELATED TO THE PRESENTLY EXISTING INJURIES, **EVEN THOUGH AT THE PRESENT TIME, SAID ADDITIONAL INJURIES ARE COMPLETELY UNKNOWN AND UNSUSPECTED.**

We further understand that the amount received in exchange for this Release is accepted not only for the injuries and damages which are now, or in the future may be, claimed to have resulted from the aforementioned incident, but is also accepted to avoid the uncertainty, expense, and delay of litigation.

We warrant that all healthcare providers have been fully paid, or will be fully paid from either the settlement proceeds or other sources. We agree to indemnify and hold the Released Parties harmless from any claims which might be asserted by such healthcare providers.

We agree the money now being paid us is fair and equitable under all circumstances and regard such payment as a full and final settlement of all claims, rights, and damages which we now have or may have against the Released Parties.

WE HAVE READ THIS RELEASE, UNDERSTAND IT, AND SIGN IT FREELY AND VOLUNTARILY.

Signed the ______ day of ____________2001, in __________________

____

JOHN DOE

____

JANE DOE

If accident-related symptoms or complications surface after settling, there may be insurance benefits available from sources other than the party with whom you settled. For instance, the medical payment benefits under your own automobile insurance policy may cover the cost of treatment if it is shown that the symptoms were caused by the accident. You may also have health insurance which covers treatment for problems which surface after settlement.

Because of the finality of settlement, it's prudent to be patient. Have every assurance from your doctor that you're medically stable and not likely to experience any further accident-related health problems. Remember that you can settle at any time prior to expiration of the statute of limitations.

Settlement of the bodily injury claim also involves payment of certain bills. Don't neglect to pay the doctor or any other creditor who's been patient enough to wait until your settlement for payment. Here's a partial checklist of considerations with regard to creditors who may need to be paid:

A. Does there exist a lien for workers' compensation benefits paid?
B. Do any health care providers have liens against the recovery?
C. Have you received Medicare benefits which are to be repaid?
D. Are any health maintenance organizations [HMO] or prepaid health plans entitled to reimbursement from the settlement?
E. Is your health and/or auto insurer entitled to reimbursement for benefits paid?

In many states, health care providers have the right to perfect medical liens by filing in the public record a notice which sets forth the amount owed, the name and address of the patient and other basic information. Check with the county recorder of your residence, under your name, for medical liens of which you may be unaware.

The benefits of a compromise or discount of the unpaid bills is discussed in Chapter Eight. Depending on who the creditor is, you may save 10% to 50% off the face amount of the bill by simply asking for it.

The question may surface whether the proceeds of settlement are taxable. Compensation for pain, anxiety and other subjective elements of your damages is not taxable. If some portion of the settlement is reimbursement for lost wages or other economic losses, that portion of the settlement is taxable.

"The will to win is important, but the will to prepare is vital."

--Joe Paterno

"It's not what an attorney tells me I may do; but what humanity, reason and justice tell me I ought to do."

--Edmund Burke

CHAPTER TEN

ATTORNEYS

Pursuing a claim without an attorney is discouraged if your injuries are serious or permanent. Troublesome liability or insurance coverage issues also indicate that legal representation is advisable. There's only one opportunity to get reimbursed for past, present and future accident-related damages.

If a lawsuit is necessary, retain an attorney. Insurance companies are in the business of litigating. They know who the best trial attorneys are and have the resources to hire them. You'd be putting yourself at an unfair and unreasonable disadvantage attempting to represent yourself in litigation. The courts would not be sympathetic if you don't know the rules and procedures of the legal process. For that matter, the courts have held in some states that unrepresented parties will be held to the same familiarity with the rules of procedure and statutes as would be attributed to qualified members of the bar.[11]

Find an attorney who knows what he/she's doing in auto claims matters. Many states certify as specialists attorneys who have demonstrated significant experience and knowledge in the personal injury claims arena. Check with your state bar for guidance. Get a list which reflects the attorneys who hold the requisite certification. Don't rely solely on Yellow Pages or other advertising in choosing an attorney.

If you need legal counsel at any stage of the claims process, talk to several attorneys by phone. If you call an attorney without an appointment, keep the conversation brief. Ask for fee information, including the cost of an initial consultation. There may be no charge or only a modest charge. You can get much valuable information in the course of a consultation if you are prepared to discuss specific issues and questions.

If you retain an attorney on a contingent fee basis, review and understand the fee agreement before signing it. The agreement will probably obligate you to pay the attorney's expenses. Find out how much they will be.

If a lawsuit is filed, the costs can be substantial. Depositions, experts, filing fees, private investigators, process servers and travel expenses can be costly. Some attorneys are willing to pay the costs and wait until the case is resolved for reimbursement. It's helpful to have an attorney with the financial resources to do this.

If the attorney proposed a thirty-three percent (33%) contingent fee, negotiate a better deal. If liability is clear and there is insurance coverage to pay for your damages, many attorneys will take the case on a lower percentage contingent fee, especially if there is a reasonable prospect that the case will settle without litigation. If you've entered a thirty-three percent (33%) contingent fee agreement in connection with a claim that settles prior to suit and with little demands on the attorney, the chances are excellent that the attorney has an ethical duty to discount the fee. As we discussed in Chapter Eight, the attorney has an ethical duty to discount the fee, whatever the fee agreement says, if literal enforcement of the agreement would result in payment of an excessive fee.

Negotiate an agreement with a sliding contingent fee by which the attorney's compensation reflects the amount of time and effort put into the case. The effort invested in a claim which settles prior to filing suit is minimal when contrasted to the number of hours which must be spent by the attorney preparing for and taking a case to trial. Fairness suggests a contingent fee of ten percent (10%) to twenty percent (20%) for a claim that settles prior to filing suit. If the case settles when litigation is pending but before trial, a higher contingent fee is appropriate. If the case actually goes to trial, the attorney will have earned a greater portion of the recovery. No reputable attorney should be offended by a proposal to negotiate the contingent fee along these lines. This is especially true if the claim involves serious damages, liability is clear and there is adequate insurance to pay the claim.

In weighing options relative to fee arrangements, consider paying the attorney by the hour to settle your claim. It may take the attorney ten to twenty hours to investigate, evaluate and negotiate a settlement. Even if you have to pay $2,000 to $3,000 for this effort, you may save thousands of dollars by avoiding payment of the contingent fee. If the case doesn't settle, economics may dictate that a contingent fee agreement makes the most sense.

The Lawyer Contingent Fee Limitation Act

In California, an attempt was made to codify the attorney's ethical duty to keep the contingent fee reasonable by a failed initiative, the Lawyer Contingent Fee Limitation Act (LCFLA). The basic idea of the initiative was to limit attorneys' contingent fees to fifteen percent (15%) of the recovery in cases that settled early. The proposed legislation was prompted by findings of the California Attorney General that:

1. The contingent-fee arrangements lawyers typically negotiate with claimants, most of whom are inexperienced and unsophisticated purchasers of legal services, often require claimants to pay their lawyers too much for handling tort claims that a defendant has offered to settle.
2. These excessive fees harm claimants by depriving them of compensation they deserve.
3. The excessive fees also discourage early settlement of tort claims, forcing injured people to suffer long delays in receiving compensation and clogging the courts with lawsuits that should not have to be filed.
4. Imposing a cap on the fees lawyers can charge for handling tort claims that a defendant has offered to settle quickly would:
   (a) Prevent lawyers from taking an unreasonable portion of the compensation offered or awarded to an injured person.
   (b) Encourage defendants to settle quickly.
   (c) Enable injured people to be compensated more promptly.
   (d) Relieve some of the present burden on the courts, reducing costs for taxpayers and enabling other legal disputes to be resolved more quickly.

The LCFLA requires that a claimant tender a "demand for compensation" to the "allegedly responsible party." The demand package is to include various materials which relate to the liability of the other party and the claimant's damages. The contents of the demand for compensation are specifically detailed in the LCFLA. These are materials that a claimant's attorney would, in any case, generally provide to another party in attempting to settle a claim.

The statute allows the allegedly responsible party to respond with an "early settlement offer" within 60 days of receipt of the demand for compensation. If the offer is accepted, the claimant's attorney may not collect contingent fees exceeding 15% of the early settlement offer. If the offer is not accepted, the statute provides:

> An attorney who represents a claimant who has rejected or failed to accept an early settlement offer shall not collect a contingent fee that is greater than 15% of the amount of the early settlement offer **plus such percentage of the amount recovered in excess of the early settlement offer as was agreed to by the claimant and the attorney.**

For example, let's assume a claimant makes a demand for compensation seeking $10,000 to settle. If the allegedly responsible party responds with an early settlement offer of $8,000 that settles the claim, the attorney's contingent fee may not exceed fifteen percent (15%) of $8,000. If the other party responds to the demand with an early settlement offer of $4,000, the claimant may reject the offer, file suit or communicate a counterproposal. If the case finally settles for $15,000, the attorney would be entitled to a contingent fee of fifteen percent (15%) of the first $4,000, the amount of the early settlement offer, plus thirty percent (30%) (or whatever other percentage is provided for in the fee agreement) of $11,000. The attorney is compensated at a higher percentage for that portion of the recovery that was disputed.

A copy of the Lawyer Contingent Fee Limitation Act is provided in the Appendix. It represents a common sense alternative to the current system that is vulnerable to abuse by attorneys. If you believe that part of the problem with lawyers is excessive fees and exploitation of the contingent fee system, send a copy of the statute to your state representative, bar association or attorney. Encourage them to consider the benefits of the system and its fairness to the consumer.

Effective Communications

Effective communications with your attorney can be crucial to a satisfactory resolution of your auto accident claim. Preparation for meetings is important. Before appointments, gather and organize all documents that pertain to the matters you will discuss. This simple step can save time and money and will help your lawyer better understand your situation.

With only a few narrow exceptions, your lawyer has an ethical obligation not to disclose to third parties the information you discuss without your permission. Almost everything you tell the lawyer and his staff is completely confidential and protected by the attorney-client privilege. The confidentiality of the attorney-client privilege allows you to be completely honest with your attorney so he/she can represent you as effectively as possible. There are a few rare exceptions to the attorney-client privilege. Such exceptions include communications to third parties which may be necessary to prevent the commission of a crime. An attorney's duty to keep your communications confidential continues even after the attorney-client relationship ends.

The attorney-client relationship involves mutual rights and responsibilities. You should expect your attorney to:

1. Represent you diligently and ethically.
2. Be competent in his or her representation.
3. Inform you periodically about the status of your case and, if you request, provide you with copies of all legal documents he or she prepares for you.

4. Return your phone calls with reasonable promptness.
5. Charge you a reasonable fee and tell you in advance the basis of that fee. He/she should also provide you with written confirmation of your fee agreement whether it is contingent, based on an hourly rate, or computed by some other method.
6. Provide an estimate of the costs and legal fees.
7. Advise you of the potential costs for which you may be responsible to the other side if your case is lost.
8. Keep confidential all statements and information that you reveal in the course of your relationship.
9. Give you the opportunity to make the ultimate decisions involving your claim including the decision whether to settle.
10. Provide you with a complete copy of your file if you or the lawyer need to end the attorney-client relationship.

You have corresponding obligations with respect to the attorney-client relationship. Your lawyer will expect you to:

1. Give him/her a truthful recitation of the facts surrounding your claim. A lawyer can only help a client when there has been full disclosure. You have the responsibility to promptly notify the lawyer of changed circumstances.
2. Give him/her prompt responses to reasonable and necessary requests.
3. Set appointments in advance. Don't show up at the lawyer's office expecting to receive a consultation.
4. Be on time for all meetings and legal proceedings.
5. Communicate with the lawyer in a timely manner if you are unhappy about the representation or have questions about your case.
6. Pay the attorney's fee in a prompt manner. If prompt payment is not possible for one reason or another, communicate with the lawyer about it.

Legal fees and costs. Some people use the terms "fees" and "costs" interchangeably. They're not the same. Fees refer to the compensation paid to the lawyer or his staff for time spent working on your case. Costs are charges incurred by your lawyer from third persons with respect to the processing or litigation of your claim. Costs may include charges by private investigators, process servers, court reporters, filing fees, experts, copying, postage and so forth.

Under the traditional contingent fee agreement, a fee is not payable to the attorney if there is no recovery. The client is nonetheless responsible to reimburse the lawyer for costs he/she has incurred in the course of the representation. The amount of such costs will vary considerably from case to case depending on the nature of your auto accident claim. Often costs are reimbursed to the lawyer from the client's share of the recovery when the claim is resolved. Insist that your lawyer contact you with an explanation if there are any major changes in his or her estimate of the costs. Your lawyer should also talk with you before making major cost expenditures such as for experts or outside consultants. Let your lawyer know that you want to be kept informed about costs as they accrue and ask your lawyer to explain options you might have for holding costs down.

After the first meeting with the lawyer, make sure you leave with answers to important questions. Some suggested questions you may want to ask your lawyer include the following:

1. What is your experience in litigating auto accident claims?
2. How many cases like mine have you handled?
3. How many cases like mine have you litigated? Taken to trial?
4. What are your rates and how will the billing be handled?
5. What is the total estimated expense for fees and costs in my case?
6. How can we keep the fees and costs down?
7. Are you willing to pay the costs then be reimbursed when my case settles?
8. If my claim is not settled, what are my litigation options?
9. What are the prospects that I will prevail if we must file a lawsuit?
10. If we lose, will I be responsible to pay certain costs incurred by the other side? If so, how much are they likely to be?
11. How will you keep me informed of the status of my case and how frequently will I hear from you?
12. If you're not available when I call, who else with your office can I contact about my case?
13. How long will it be before my claim is settled? If a lawsuit is necessary, how long does that process take?

Small Claims Court

The point has been made that representing oneself in litigation is not wise. Even for attorneys, the age-old maxim that "he who represents himself has a fool for a client" is valid. There are too many pitfalls in doing battle with the insurance company's attorney. An exception to the general admonition against representing oneself is for Small Claims Court proceedings.

Most court systems have a Small Claims Court division for the inexpensive processing of small claims. The jurisdiction of the Small Claims Court varies from state to state. If, after investigation and careful analysis, the value of your claim has been determined to be within the jurisdiction of the Small Claims Court, there is no reason not to sue if the insurance company has been unreasonable in refusing to settle.

In most states, attorneys are not permitted to practice in the Small Claims Court. However, there is a mechanism in many states for removal of a case from the Small Claims Court division to a higher level where attorneys are permitted to practice. Thus, no matter how little may be in controversy, if the person you have sued insists on having legal counsel, you may end up back on that uneven playing field. Nonetheless, with nothing ventured, there is nothing gained.

The Small Claims Court system is generally set up with user-friendly forms. The process is inexpensive and accelerated. It is possible to get before a judge for a hearing in a few months. What goes on during the hearing tends to be informal. The technical rules of court are relaxed. There is generally no appeal from the judge's decision in Small Claims Court cases.

"Money talks...but does it tell the truth?"

--Author Unknown

"Man's mind, stretched to a new idea,
never goes back to its original dimensions."

--Oliver Wendell Holmes

AFTERWORD

Not even the most skilled and experienced attorney has the answer to every question which is likely to surface in asserting a claim. Attorneys are trained to gather facts by asking questions and identifying key issues. Hopefully, this publication will sensitize you to the more important questions that must be asked and answered to successfully navigate the claims process.

The journey will be a challenge. You will be dealing with an insurance adjuster who has been trained and probably has considerable experience, often dealing with attorneys. A healthy caution of the task at hand should be balanced with determination, a willingness to learn, and patience. Hard work and preparation instill confidence. Whether you have any legal experience or not, you can work harder than the other side in preparing the claim for settlement.

Although one of the objectives of this book is to limit the involvement and expense of attorneys in the settlement process, some legal counsel may be indispensable to a positive result. Even if you pay for several hours of legal counsel to resolve the claim, you will be many dollars ahead if the much more expensive contingent fee can be avoided.

If the claim is problematic, damages serious, or litigation inevitable, find a good attorney. You have some practical guidelines for knowing when legal representation is appropriate and how to negotiate a fair fee agreement.

We learn by doing, and we learn from our mistakes. Hopefully, through the use of this book, your mistakes will be small ones. The first step, the next one, is up to you.

As you evaluate, investigate, and negotiate your claim, refer to this manual often. Make notes in it. Tell me your experiences. Let me know where this book may be improved. When your claim has been settled and justice served, tell me about your success.

Good luck.

END NOTES

1 28 USCA sec. 1346

2 Restatement, Second, Torts sec. 282, 283

3 65 Corpus Juris Secundum, Negligence sec. 2(1)

4 *City of Tucson v. Holliday*, 3 Ariz.App. 10, 21, 411 P2d 183 (App., 1966)

5 Jackson, R. *The Cervical Syndrome*, Fourth Edition, 1977

6 Omer PA: *A Physician -Engineer s View of Low Velocity Rear End Collisions*, SAE Technical Paper Series (1992)

7 Croft, Arthur C., DC, MSc, FACO, *Whiplash Injuries and Low Speed Collisions: Confessions of an Accident Reconstructionist*, FORUM, Consumer Attorneys of California, July/August 1997

8 Ameis A, *Cervical Whiplash: Considerations in the Rehabilitation of Cervical Myofascial Injury*, Can Fam Phys, 32:1871-76, September 1 1986

9 Id.

10 *In the Matter of a Member of the State Bar of Arizona, John F. Swartz, respondent*, 141 Ariz. 266, 686 P2d 1236 (1984)

11 7 Corpus Juris Secundum, Attorney & Client

APPENDIX

AUTO ACCIDENT CLAIM CHECKLIST

At the Accident Scene

* Get the other driver's name, address, telephone number, and insurance company name and policy number.
* Get the names, addresses, and phone numbers of any witnesses.
* Get the name of the police officer who comes to the scene of the accident. Ask when and where a copy of the accident report will be available.
* Get medical attention right away, regardless of whether you think you've been injured. Often, symptoms from an injury will not surface for several days.
* Write down everything you can remember about the accident as soon as possible. Draw a diagram of the streets, the direction of the vehicles, location of witnesses, and any other details you can recall.
* Take pictures of the accident scene, if possible, before any of the vehicles have been removed.

---

* Calendar expiration of statute of limitations.
* Name, address, and phone number of claims adjuster for other party.
* Was the other party on the job at the time of the accident? If so, investigate identity and insurance coverage of employer.
* Find out how much liability coverage the other party has.
* If the other party is uninsured or underinsured, check uninsured or underinsured coverages under your own policy and put your insurer on notice of claim.
* Get a copy of the accident report.
* Determine whether the other party was cited.
* Determine what court the traffic citation will be tried in, if contested.
* If the other party pleads guilty or accepts responsibility, get evidence of same from the court.
* If the other party contests the traffic complaint, plan to attend the hearing with a court reporter.
* Get statements from all witnesses who are helpful.
* Photograph damage to the vehicle.
* Investigate damage to the vehicle which may not be apparent from

photos; i.e., to the undercarriage and frame or damage to mechanical functions of the vehicle.

* Photograph visible evidence of personal injuries.
* Investigate benefits such as health insurance, disability insurance, workers' compensation, and medical payment benefits under your auto insurance policy.
* Obtain copies of all relevant insurance policies with endorsements and declarations sheets.
* If benefits are to be paid by insurance providers, determine whether they are entitled to reimbursement from the settlement.
* Document lost wages with detailed letter from employer.
* Assemble a list of every physician and health care provider who treated you.
* From each doctor and health care provider, obtain complete copies of medical records and itemized invoices.
* Obtain a brief narrative report from primary treating physician which includes diagnosis, prognosis and statement that injury was caused by the accident.
* Maintain a journal which describes accident-related pain, discomfort, and impact of symptoms on lifestyle.
* Document all communications with insurance adjuster; prepare confirming letters as necessary.
* Settle property damage claim first, but settle bodily injury claim only after the doctor releases you and you know what your claim is worth.
* If preexisting injury is an issue, obtain all relevant medical records from prior to the accident.
* Seek guidance from legal counsel on a limited basis for issues that arise.
* Communicate with unpaid health care providers in writing and formalize lien agreements if necessary.
* Prior to settling, ask health care providers to reduce their claims against the recovery.
* Prior to settling, ask insurance companies who have paid benefits to reduce their liens, if any.
* If the case is problematic or damages serious or permanent, seek legal counsel.
* If the case is not settled ninety (90) days prior to expiration of statute of limitations, seek legal counsel.

STATUTES OF LIMITATION

ALABAMA
2 YEARS (Ala. Code sec. 6-2-38)

ALASKA
2 years (Alaska Stat. sec. 09.10.070)

ARIZONA
2 years (Ariz. Rev. Stat. Ann. sec. 12-542)

ARKANSAS
5 years (Ark. Stat.Ann. sec. 16-56-115)

CALIFORNIA
1 year (Cal. Code of Civ. Proc. sec 340)

COLORADO
2 years (Colo. Rev. Stat. sec. 13-80-102)

CONNECTICUT
2 years (Conn. Gen. Stat. Ann. sec. 52-584)

DELAWARE
2 years (Del. Code Ann. sec. 8107, sec. 8119)

DISTRICT OF COLUMBIA
3 years (D.C. Code Ann. sec. 12-301)

FLORIDA
4 years (Fla. Stat. Ann. sec. 95.11)

GEORGIA
2 years (Ga. Code Ann. sec. 3-1004)

HAWAII
2 years (Hawaii Rev. Stat. sec. 657-7)

IDAHO
2 years (Idaho Code sec. 5-219)

ILLINOIS
2 years (Ill. Ann. Stat., sec. 13-202)

INDIANA
2 years (Ind. Code Ann. sec. 34-1-2-2)

IOWA
2 years (Iowa Code Ann. sec. 614.1)

KANSAS
2 years (Kan. Stat. Ann. sec. 60-513)

KENTUCKY
1 year (Ky. Rev. Stat. sec. 413.140)

LOUISIANA
1 year (La. Civ. Code Ann. art. 3492)

MAINE
6 years (Me. Rev. Stat. Ann. art. 14, sec. 752)

MARYLAND
3 years (Md. Ann. Code sec. 5-101)

MASSACHUSETTS
3 years (Mass. Gen. Laws Ann. art. 260, sec. 2A,4)

MICHIGAN
3 years (Mich. Comp. Laws sec. 600.5805)

MINNESOTA
2 years (Minn. Stat. Ann. sec 541.07)

MISSISSIPPI
3 years (Miss. Code Ann. sec. 15-1-49)

MISSOURI
5 years (Mo. Ann. Stat. title 35, sec. 516.120)

MONTANA
3 years (Mont. Code Ann. Sec. 27-2-204, 207)

NEBRASKA
4 years (Neb. Rev. Stat. sec. 25-207)

NEVADA
2 years (Nev. Rev. Stat. Ann. sec. 11.190)

NEW HAMPSHIRE
3 years (N.H. Rev. Stat. Ann. sec. 508:4)

NEW JERSEY
2 years (N.J. Stat. Ann. sec. 2A:14-2)

NEW MEXICO
3 years (N.M. Stat. Ann. sec. 37-1-8)

NEW YORK
3 years (N.Y. Civ. Prac. R sec. 214)

NORTH CAROLINA
3 years (N.C. Gen. Stat. sec. 1-52)

NORTH DAKOTA
6 years (N.D. Cent. Code sec. 28-01-16)

OHIO
2 years (Ohio Rev. Code Ann. sec. 2305.10)

OKLAHOMA
2 years (Okla. Stat. Ann. Title 12, sec. 95)

OREGON
2 years (Or. Rev. Stat. sec. 12.110[1])

PENNSYLVANIA
2 years (42 Pa. Con. Stat. Ann. 42, sec. 5524)

RHODE ISLAND
3 years (R.I. Gen. Laws. Sec. 9-1-14)

SOUTH CAROLINA
3 years (S.C. Code Ann. Sec. 15-3-530)

SOUTH DAKOTA
3 years (S.D. Comp. Laws Ann., sec. 15-2-12.2, 15-2-14)

TENNESSEE
1 year (Tenn. Code Ann. sec. 28-3-104)

TEXAS
2 years (Tex. Civ. Prac. & Rem. Code. Title 2, sec. 16.003)

UTAH
4 years (Utah Code Ann. Sec. 78-12-25[3])

VERMONT
3 years (Vt. Stat. Ann. Title 12, sec. 512)

VIRGINIA
2 years (Va. Code, sec. 8.01-243)

WASHINGTON
3 years (Wash. Rev. Code Ann., sec. 4.16.020)

WEST VIRGINIA
2 years (W. Va. Code sec. 55-2-12)

WISCONSIN
3 years (Wis. Stat. Ann. sec. 893.54)

WYOMING
4 years (Wyo. Stat. Ann. sec. 1-3-105)

ADOT USE ONLY

ARIZONA TRAFFIC ACCIDENT REPORT

1 *POLICE ONLY* - FORWARD COPY TO ADOT TRAFFIC RECORDS SECTION 064R 206 S 17th AVE, PHOENIX, ARIZONA 85007-3233

REPORT ID: YEAR | MONTH | DAY | HOUR | NCIC NO. | OFFICERS ID NO.

Agency Report Number

Total No. of Sheets ____

COMPLETE THE FOLLOWING SUPPLEMENT IF ANY ✓ (circle) *AND* ANY ✓ (diamond) ARE CHECKED

2 Total Units | Total Injuries | Total Fatalities | Estimated Total Damage Compared to Limit: ☐ Over ☐ Under | ○ Fatal ☐ Hit/Run | ☐ Govt. Prop. | ○ Persons Transported for Immediate Medical Care? | ○ Tow Away of At Least One Vehicle from Scene? | District or Grid No.

3 LOCATION

On Highway/Road / Street | ☐ Inside ☐ Outside | City | County

Intersecting Street, Road / M.P. or R.P. ☐ At ☐ From | ☐ North ☐ East ☐ South ☐ West | ☐ Plus ☐ Minus | Distance | ☐ Measured ☐ Approximate | ☐ Miles ☐ Feet

4

TRAFFIC UNIT NO. ____

State | Class | End. | ☐ DL # | ☐ SSN | ☐ Both | ☐ Driver ☐ Pedestrian ☐ Pedalcyclist | Name | Sex | Inj

Restrictions | Date of Birth | Address | City | State | Zip Code | Telephone Number

Plate Number | State | Year | ☐ Same as Driver | Owner/Carrier Name | Address | City | State | Zip Code

Body Style | ◇ Bus (9 or more seats) | Make | Color | Year | VIN | Safety Device Code

Removed to | ☐ Disabled ☐ Not Disabled | Removed by | Orders of | Posted Speed Limit | Ofc Est Speed

Insurance Company | Telephone Number | Policy Number | Eff Date / Exp Date

Trailer (Other Unit) Plate No. | State | Year | Description of Trailer or Other Unit | GVW (Registered) of Power Unit Greater than 10k pounds? ◇ Yes ☐ No | HazMat Placard? ◇ Yes ☐ No 4-Digit 1-Digit | Was HazMat Cargo Released? ☐ Yes ☐ No

TRAFFIC UNIT NO. ____

State | Class | End. | ☐ DL # | ☐ SSN | ☐ Both | ☐ Driver ☐ Pedestrian ☐ Pedalcyclist | Name | Sex | Inj

Restrictions | Date of Birth | Address | City | State | Zip Code | Telephone Number

Plate Number | State | Year | ☐ Same as Driver | Owner/Carrier Name | Address | City | State | Zip Code

Body Style | ◇ Bus (9 or more seats) | Make | Color | Year | VIN | Safety Device Code

Removed to | ☐ Disabled ☐ Not Disabled | Removed by | Orders of | Posted Speed Limit | Ofc Est Speed

Insurance Company | Telephone Number | Policy Number | Eff Date / Exp Date

Trailer (Other Unit) Plate No. | State | Year | Description of Trailer or Other Unit | GVW (Registered) of Power Unit Greater than 10k pounds? ◇ Yes ☐ No | HazMat Placard? ◇ Yes ☐ No 4-Digit 1-Digit | Was HazMat Cargo Released? ☐ Yes ☐ No

TRAFFIC UNIT NO. ____

State | Class | End. | ☐ DL # | ☐ SSN | ☐ Both | ☐ Driver ☐ Pedestrian ☐ Pedalcyclist | Name | Sex | Inj

Restrictions | Date of Birth | Address | City | State | Zip Code | Telephone Number

Plate Number | State | Year | ☐ Same as Driver | Owner/Carrier Name | Address | City | State | Zip Code

Body Style | ◇ Bus (9 or more seats) | Make | Color | Year | VIN | Safety Device Code

Removed to | ☐ Disabled ☐ Not Disabled | Removed by | Orders of | Posted Speed Limit | Ofc Est Speed

Insurance Company | Telephone Number | Policy Number | Eff Date / Exp Date

Trailer (Other Unit) Plate No. | State | Year | Description of Trailer or Other Unit | GVW (Registered) of Power Unit Greater than 10k pounds? ◇ Yes ☐ No | HazMat Placard? ◇ Yes ☐ No 4-Digit 1-Digit | Was HazMat Cargo Released? ☐ Yes ☐ No

5 PASSENGERS

Seating Position

07	04	01
08	05	02
09	06	03

10 Not in Passenger Compart.
11 Motorcycle, Bus
12 Other
13 Unknown
14 Pedalcyclist

Safety Devices
1 None used
2 Lap belt
3 Lap & shoulder
4 Airbag deployed
5 Child restraint
6 Protective helmet
7 Passive belt
8 Passive & lap
9 Other
0 Unknown

Injury Severity Codes
1 - No injury
2 - Possible injury
3 - Non Incapacitating Injury
4 - Incapacitating Injury
5 - Fatal Injury
6 - Not Reported / Unknown

Unit #	Seat Pos	SD	Name	Address	City	State	Zip Code	Age	Sex	Inj

6 Other Property Damage (Describe)

Owner's Name | Address | City | State | Zip Code | Telephone Number

7 WITNESSES

Name	Address	City	State	Zip Code	Telephone Number	Age

8 Photos Taken ☐ Yes ☐ No | Photographer's Name, ID Number and Agency | Invest at Scene ☐ Yes ☐ No | Date Invest | Time Invest

Officer's Signature and ID Number | Agency | Date Completed

01-2704 R06/00

9 - DIAGRAM

10 - INDICATE NORTH

11 - SKIDDING OCCURRED

	VEHICLE 1	2	3
YES	☐	☐	☐
NO	☐	☐	☐

12 - CITATIONS
UNIT NO. A.R.S. NO. OR CITY CODE

14 - PRIOR ACTION
☐ YES ☐ NO RAN OFF ROADWAY PRIOR TO FIRST HARMFUL EVENT
☐ RIGHT ☐ LEFT UNIT NO. ________

15 - MANNER OF COLLISION
CHECK ONLY ONE
1 ☐ SINGLE VEHICLE
2 ☐ ANGLE
3 ☐ LEFT TURN
4 ☐ RIGHT TURN
5 ☐ U-TURN
6 ☐ REAR-END
7 ☐ HEAD-ON
8 ☐ SIDESWIPE (SAME DIRECTION)
9 ☐ SIDESWIPE (OPPOSITE DIRECTION)
10 ☐ BACKING
11 ☐ NON-CONTACT MOTORCYCLE
12 ☐ NON-CONTACT NON-MOTORCYCLE
13 ☐ PEDESTRIAN
14 ☐ PEDALCYCLE
15 ☐ OTHER

13 - DESCRIBE WHAT HAPPENED

INJURED TAKEN TO / BY

16 - LIGHT CONDITION
CHECK ONLY ONE
1 ☐ DAYLIGHT
2 ☐ DAWN OR DUSK
3 ☐ DARKNESS

YES NO
1 ☐ ☐ STREETLIGHT
2 ☐ ☐ STREETLIGHT FUNCTIONING

17 - WEATHER CONDITIONS
CHECK ONLY ONE
1 ☐ CLEAR
2 ☐ CLOUDY
3 ☐ SLEET / HAIL
4 ☐ RAIN
5 ☐ SNOW
6 ☐ SEVERE CROSSWINDS
7 ☐ BLOWING SAND, SOIL, DIRT, SNOW
8 ☐ FOG, SMOG, SMOKE

18 - ROAD SURFACE TYPE
CHECK ONLY ONE
1 ☐ ASPHALT
2 ☐ CONCRETE
3 ☐ GRAVEL
4 ☐ DIRT
5 ☐ OTHER

19 - TYPE OF LOCATION
CHECK ONLY ONE
1 ☐ INTERSECTION
2 ☐ JUNCTION AREA
3 ☐ NON-JUNCTION AREA
4 ☐ DRIVEWAY ACCESS
5 ☐ ALLEY ACCESS
6 ☐ ALLEY

20 - INTERSECTION RELATED
YES ☐ NO ☐

21 - SPECIAL LOCATION
CHECK ONLY ONE
1 ☐ SCHOOL CROSSING
2 ☐ PEDESTRIAN CROSSWALK (STRIPED)
3 ☐ PEDESTRIAN CROSSWALK (NO STRIPING)
4 ☐ BRIDGE
5 ☐ TUNNEL
6 ☐ RR CROSSING
7 ☐ GORE AREA
8 ☐ BIKE PATH
9 ☐ 2-WAY LEFT TURN LANE

22 - UNUSUAL ROAD CONDITION
CHECK ONLY ONE
1 ☐ UNDER CONSTRUCTION, TRAFFIC ALLOWED
2 ☐ UNDER CONSTRUCTION, NO TRAFFIC ALLOWED
3 ☐ UNDER REPAIRS
4 ☐ HOLES, RUTS, BUMPS
5 ☐ OBSTRUCTION - PROTECTED
6 ☐ OBSTRUCTION - UNPROTECTED
7 ☐ OBSTRUCTION - UNLIGHTED AT NIGHT
8 ☐ DEFECTIVE SHOULDERS
9 ☐ CHANGING ROAD WIDTH
10 ☐ WATER (STANDING OR MOVING)
11 ☐ TEMPORARY LANE CLOSURE

23 - TRAFFIC CONTROL DEVICES
LEGEND:
A-DEVICE OPERATIONAL
B-DAMAGED OR NON-FUNCTIONAL PRIOR TO ACCIDENT
CHECK ANY THAT APPLY

	A	B	
1	☐	☐	TRAFFIC SIGNAL
2	☐	☐	YIELD SIGN
3	☐	☐	STOP SIGN
4	☐	☐	WARNING SIGN
5	☐	☐	RAILROAD SIGNAL
6	☐	☐	FLASHING SIGNAL
7	☐	☐	FLAGMAN OR OFFICER

24 - NON-INTERSECTION ROAD CHARACTER
CHECK ONLY ONE
1 ☐ 2-WAY STRIPED CENTERLINE
2 ☐ 2-WAY, NO STRIPE
3 ☐ 2-WAY, PAINTED MEDIAN
4 ☐ 2-WAY, RAISED MEDIAN
5 ☐ 2-WAY, CONCRETE BARRIER
6 ☐ 2-WAY, CABLE BARRIER
7 ☐ 2-WAY, DEPRESSED MEDIAN
8 ☐ 2-WAY EXTENDED MEDIAN
9 ☐ 1-WAY STREET

25 - ROAD GRADE
CHECK ONLY ONE
1 ☐ LEVEL
2 ☐ DOWNGRADE
3 ☐ UPGRADE
4 ☐ HILLCREST
5 ☐ DIP

26 - ROAD SURFACE CONDITION
CHECK ONLY ONE
1 ☐ DRY
2 ☐ WET
3 ☐ SAND, MUD, DIRT, OIL, GRAVEL
4 ☐ SNOW
5 ☐ SLUSH
6 ☐ ICE
7 ☐ OTHER
8 ☐ UNKNOWN

27 - CONDITIONS INFLUENCING DRIVER
TWO CHOICES PER PERSON MAY BE SELECTED

	1	2	3	
1	☐	☐	☐	NO APPARENT INFLUENCE
2	☐	☐	☐	HAD BEEN DRINKING
3	☐	☐	☐	USE OF ILLICIT DRUGS
4	☐	☐	☐	ILLNESS
5	☐	☐	☐	FELL ASLEEP / FATIGUED
6	☐	☐	☐	PHYSICAL IMPAIRMENT
7	☐	☐	☐	PRESCRIPTION DRUGS
8	☐	☐	☐	OTHER
9	☐	☐	☐	UNKNOWN

28 - VIOLATIONS / BEHAVIOR
TWO CHOICES PER PERSON MAY BE SELECTED

	1	2	3	
1	☐	☐	☐	NO IMPROPER ACTION
2	☐	☐	☐	SPEED TOO FAST FOR CONDITIONS
3	☐	☐	☐	EXCEEDED LAWFUL SPEED
4	☐	☐	☐	FAILED TO YIELD RIGHT-OF-WAY
5	☐	☐	☐	FOLLOWED TOO CLOSELY
6	☐	☐	☐	RAN STOP SIGN
7	☐	☐	☐	DISREGARDED TRAFFIC SIGNAL
8	☐	☐	☐	MADE IMPROPER TURN
9	☐	☐	☐	DROVE IN OPPOSING TRAFFIC LANE
10	☐	☐	☐	KNOWINGLY OPERATED WITH FAULTY OR MISSING EQUIPMENT
11	☐	☐	☐	REQUIRED MOTORCYCLE SAFETY EQUIPMENT NOT USED
12	☐	☐	☐	PASSED IN NO PASSING ZONE
13	☐	☐	☐	UNSAFE LANE CHANGE
14	☐	☐	☐	OTHER UNSAFE PASSING
15	☐	☐	☐	INATTENTION
16	☐	☐	☐	DID NOT USE CROSSWALK
17	☐	☐	☐	WALKED ON WRONG SIDE OF ROAD
18	☐	☐	☐	OTHER
19	☐	☐	☐	UNKNOWN

29 - VEHICLE CONDITION
TWO CHOICES PER VEHICLE MAY BE SELECTED

	1	2	3	
1	☐	☐	☐	NO APPARENT DEFECTS
2	☐	☐	☐	DEFECTIVE BRAKES
3	☐	☐	☐	DEFECTIVE STEERING
4	☐	☐	☐	DEFECTIVE HEADLIGHTS
5	☐	☐	☐	DEFECTIVE TAIL LIGHTS
6	☐	☐	☐	DEFECTIVE TURN-SIGNAL
7	☐	☐	☐	PUNCTURE OR BLOWOUT
8	☐	☐	☐	ONE OR MORE SMOOTH TIRES
9	☐	☐	☐	FIRE
10	☐	☐	☐	DEFECTIVE WINDSHIELD WIPER
11	☐	☐	☐	DEFECTIVE EXHAUST SYSTEM
12	☐	☐	☐	OTHER DEFECTS
13	☐	☐	☐	NO TRAILER BRAKES
14	☐	☐	☐	UNKNOWN

30 - TRAFFIC UNIT ACTION
CHECK ONE PER UNIT

	1	2	3	
1	☐	☐	☐	GOING STRAIGHT AHEAD
2	☐	☐	☐	SLOWING IN TRAFFICWAY
3	☐	☐	☐	STOPPED IN TRAFFICWAY
4	☐	☐	☐	MAKING LEFT TURN
5	☐	☐	☐	MAKING RIGHT TURN
6	☐	☐	☐	MAKING U TURN
7	☐	☐	☐	ENTERING ALLEY OR DRIVEWAY
8	☐	☐	☐	LEAVING ALLEY OR DRIVEWAY
9	☐	☐	☐	OVERTAKING/PASSING
10	☐	☐	☐	CHANGING LANES
11	☐	☐	☐	BACKING
12	☐	☐	☐	AVOIDING VEHICLE, OBJECT, PEDESTRIAN
13	☐	☐	☐	ENTERING PARKING POSITION
14	☐	☐	☐	LEAVING PARKING POSITION
15	☐	☐	☐	PROPERLY PARKED
16	☐	☐	☐	IMPROPERLY PARKED
17	☐	☐	☐	DRIVERLESS MOVING VEHICLE
18	☐	☐	☐	CROSSING ROAD
19	☐	☐	☐	WALKING WITH TRAFFIC
20	☐	☐	☐	WALKING AGAINST TRAFFIC
21	☐	☐	☐	STANDING
22	☐	☐	☐	LYING
23	☐	☐	☐	GETTING ON OR OFF VEHICLE
24	☐	☐	☐	WORKING ON OR PUSHING VEHICLE
25	☐	☐	☐	WORKING ON ROAD
26	☐	☐	☐	OTHER
27	☐	☐	☐	UNKNOWN

31 - VISION OBSCUREMENT
CHECK ONE PER UNIT

	1	2	3	
1	☐	☐	☐	NOT OBSCURED
2	☐	☐	☐	BY PARKED / STOPPED VEHICLE
3	☐	☐	☐	BY MOVING VEHICLE
4	☐	☐	☐	BY BUILDING
5	☐	☐	☐	BY EMBANKMENT
6	☐	☐	☐	BY SIGNBOARD
7	☐	☐	☐	BY HILLCREST
8	☐	☐	☐	BY LOAD ON VEHICLE
9	☐	☐	☐	BY TREES, BUSHES
10	☐	☐	☐	BY HEADLIGHT
11	☐	☐	☐	BY SUN GLARE
12	☐	☐	☐	BECAUSE OF BAD WEATHER
13	☐	☐	☐	OTHER
14	☐	☐	☐	RAIN, SNOW, FOG ON WINDSHIELD
15	☐	☐	☐	WINDSHIELD OBSCURED - OTHER
16	☐	☐	☐	UNKNOWN

32 - DIRECTION OF TRAVEL
CHECK ONE PER UNIT

	1	2	3			1	2	3	
1	☐	☐	☐	NORTH	5	☐	☐	☐	NW
2	☐	☐	☐	SOUTH	6	☐	☐	☐	NE
3	☐	☐	☐	EAST	7	☐	☐	☐	SW
4	☐	☐	☐	WEST	8	☐	☐	☐	SE
					9	☐	☐	☐	UNKNOWN

01-2704 R6/00 BACK

ARIZONA TRAFFIC ACCIDENT REPORT **SUPPLEMENT** FORWARD COPY TO ACCIDENT RECORDS ANALYSIS UNIT 064R ARIZONA DEPARTMENT OF TRANSPORTATION 206 S. 17th AVE., PHOENIX, ARIZONA 85007-3233	YEAR	MONTH	DAY	REPORT ID HOUR	NCIC NO.	OFFICERS ID NO.	Agency Report Number

ACCIDENT DIAGRAM

☐ MEASUREMENTS ARE APPROXIMATE AND NOT TO SCALE

☐ MEASUREMENTS ARE SCALED (SCALE = ____________

INDICATE NORTH

† ● 01-2708 2/92
FORM A

ARIZONA TRAFFIC ACCIDENT REPORT
SUPPLEMENT
FORWARD COPY TO
ACCIDENT RECORDS ANALYSIS UNIT 064R
ARIZONA DEPARTMENT OF TRANSPORTATION
206 S. 17th AVE., PHOENIX, ARIZONA 85007-3233

REPORT ID						Agency Report Number
YEAR	MONTH	DAY	HOUR	NCIC NO.	OFFICERS ID NO.	

ACCIDENT DESCRIPTION
(Narrative)

INVESTIGATOR'S SIGNATURE DATE

† 01-2706 2/92 (BACK)
FORM A

DOCTOR'S LIEN

TO: Insurance Carrier

RE: Patient
Doctor
Date of Accident

I give a lien to the doctor on any settlement I may receive as a result of the accident and authorize you to pay directly to the doctor such sums as may be due and owing for service rendered to me, and to withhold sums from the settlement as may be necessary to pay the doctor.

I understand that I am directly responsible to the doctor for all bills submitted by him for service rendered to me, and that this agreement is made solely for the doctor's additional protection and in consideration of his awaiting payment. I further understand that payment to the doctor is not contingent on any settlement.

Dated: Patient's signature:

AUTHORIZATION FOR RELEASE OF MEDICAL RECORDS

TO: ______________________________

RE: ______________________________

You are hereby authorized to release to me all of the following:

Medical records, including patient's record cards, x-rays, x-ray readings and reports, laboratory records and reports, all tests of any type and character and reports thereof, statements of charges, and any and all of my records pertaining to medical care, history, condition, treatment, diagnosis, prognosis, etiology or expense.

You are further authorized and directed to furnish me with oral and written reports as requested on any of the foregoing matters.

Please also send me copies of all medical and hospital bills. If there is a recovery pursuant to a settlement or after a trial, I promise to withhold an amount sufficient to pay these bills and will pay them promptly.

I hereby acknowledge that I will in no way hold you responsible, legally or otherwise, for furnishing the above pursuant to this consent and authorization. A photocopy of this form will have the same effect as the original.

DATED this _____ day of ________________________2001.

PATIENT: ____

LOSS OF FUNCTION ASSESSMENT

Directions: Check the statement that best pertains to you in each of the following categories.

SELF CARE AND PERSONAL HYGIENE CARE: *(Washing, dressing, eating, bathing, urination, defecation, brushing teeth, brushing hair)*

❑ I can provide for myself in a normal fashion.

❑ I can provide for myself but it creates pain.

❑ In providing for myself I am slow, careful and it is painful.

❑ I can manage most of my personal care but it requires some help.

❑ In most accommodations of my self care, I require help daily.

❑ I have difficulty bathing, I stay in bed and do not dress myself.

NORMAL LIVING POSTURES: *(Sitting)*

❑ I am able to assume a seated position in any chair without restriction.

❑ I am limited to one comfortable chair without restrictions.

❑ I am restricted to one hour of sitting due to pain.

❑ Due to pain, I am only able to sit for 30 minutes.

❑ Pain restricts sitting for longer than 10 minutes.

❑ I am unable to sit due to pain.

NORMAL LIVING POSTURES: *(Standing)*

❑ I am able to stand as long as I like.

❑ I am able to stand as long as I like without restrictions.

❑ I am restricted to one hour of standing due to pain.

❑ Due to pain, I am only able to stand for 30 minutes.

❑ Pain restricts standing for longer than 10 minutes.

❑ I am unable to stand due to pain.

NORMAL LIVING POSTURES: *(Lifting)*

- ❑ I am able to lift heavy weights.
- ❑ Due to pain, I am unable to lift heavy weights; however, light to medium weights at table height are manageable.
- ❑ I am able to lift heavy weights. but it causes pain.
- ❑ Pain restricts lifting to only very light weights.
- ❑ I am unable to lift heavy weights off the floor; however, if they are at table height, I can manage.
- ❑ I am unable to lift or carry.

AMBULATION: *(Walking, climbing stairs)*

- ❑ I am able to walk any distance without pain restriction.
- ❑ Due to pain, I am restricted to walks of less than 1/4 mile.
- ❑ I am limited to walks of .one mile due to pain restrictions.
- ❑ I require the use of crutches or a cane to assist walking.
- ❑ I am limited to 1/2 mile of walking due to pain.
- ❑ I remain in bed for the most part.

TRAVEL: *(Driving, flying, riding)*

- ❑ I am able to travel anywhere without restriction.
- ❑ Due to pain, I am limited to travel time of less than one hour.
- ❑ I am able to travel almost anywhere but it causes pain.
- ❑ Only short, urgent trips are possible due to pain limitations.
- ❑ I can manage two hours of travel but pain is present.
- ❑ I am restricted in travel due to pain other than emergencies or short distances (hospital, doctor)

NON-SPECIALIZED HAND ACTIVITIES:
(Grasping, lifting, tactile discrimination)

- ❑ I can grasp and lift in a normal fashion.
- ❑ Grip strength, lifting and tactile sensations are restricted by pain.
- ❑ My grip and lift capabilities are normal but always painful.
- ❑ Pain seriously limits my ability to grip and lift.
- ❑ Pain prevents grasping, lifting and tactile discrimination.

SEXUAL FUNCTION:

- ❑ I am able to engage in normal sexual activities without pain
- ❑ I am restricted in sexual activities due to pain.
- ❑ I am able to participate sexually but it creates some pain.
- ❑ Pain has created a near absent sex life.
- ❑ I engage normally in sexual activities but it is very painful.
- ❑ Due to pain, I abstain from any sexual activities.

SLEEP:

- ❑ I sleep well in a normal fashion.
- ❑ I fail to realize 4 hours of sleep, even when taking sleeping pills.
- ❑ Sleep well when I use sleeping pills without restrictions.
- ❑ I fail to realize 2 hours of sleep, even when taking sleeping pills.
- ❑ I fail to realize 6 hours sleep, even when taking sleeping pills.
- ❑ Pain prevents sleep.

SOCIAL AND RECREATIONAL ACTIVITIES:

- ❑ I am enjoying a normal, active social life with no restrictions.
- ❑ I have restrictions socially in that I do not go out as often due to pain.
- ❑ I participate in a normal social life but pain is increased during activity.
- ❑ I am restricted to social activities at home due to pain.
- ❑ The presence of pain effects the more energetic components of my social life (bowling, golfing, dancing, sports, etc.)
- ❑ Due to pain, I have no social life.

THE EFFECTS OF MEDICATION:

- ❑ I am able to tolerate my pain and use no painkillers.
- ❑ Use pain killers for moderate pain relief.
- ❑ I use no pain killers; even though pain is bad, I tolerate it.
- ❑ My pain killers offer little relief from pain.
- ❑ I use pain killers and experience complete relief of pain.
- ❑ Pain killers fail to offer relief, therefore, I no longer use them.

PAIN INTENSITY:

- ❑ My pain is MINIMAL and tolerated. It is annoying but does not impair my performance.
- ❑ Pain is SLIGHT and tolerated, but it causes some impairment in my physical performance.
- ❑ I experience MODERATE pain which causes a marked impairment in my physical performance of activities.
- ❑ I experience MARKED pain which precludes any activity.

PAIN FREQUENCY:

- ❑ I have INTERMITTENT symptoms occurring less than 25% of my awake time.
- ❑ I experience OCCASIONAL symptoms between 25% and 50% of my awake time.
- ❑ Pain is FREQUENT and occurs between 50% and 75% of my awake time.
- ❑ I have CONSTANT pain occurring between 75% and 100% of my awake time.

YOUR LETTERHEAD

Street Address
City, State Zip
Phone ____________
Fax ____________
E-mail ______________

SAMPLE FORM LETTER
TO REQUEST
COMPROMISE OF MEDICAL LIEN

Date

Flagstaff Medical Center
1200 Beaver Street
Flagstaff, Arizona 86001

RE: ACCOUNT #12345

Dear Sir or Madam:

I was involved in an automobile accident on May 18, 2000. At the time of the accident, I had no health insurance. I owe your facility more than $10,000 for accident-related treatment.

Liability for the accident is highly disputed by the parties responsible for it. A lawsuit has not been filed and I would like to avoid litigation if possible for many reasons. A lawsuit would delay a final resolution of my claim and payment to you for at least a year and possibly much longer.

If you would agree to discount your bill to $5,000, the prospects of settlement would be greatly enhanced and I believe I could get you paid within the next thirty (30) days.

I appreciate your consideration in this regard. Please contact me at your convenience to discuss satisfaction of your lien.

Thank you.

Sincerely,

Your Name

YOUR LETTERHEAD

Street Address
City, State Zip
Phone ____________
Fax ____________
E-mail ______________

SAMPLE FORM LETTER
TO REQUEST
MEDICAL RECORDS

Date

Dr. John Doe
123 Main Street
Cedarville, USA 12345

Dear Dr. Doe:

I was in an automobile accident that occurred on May 1, 1998. You may recall that you rendered treatment for my injuries. Please provide me with a complete copy of all records in your possession including an itemized statement of all charges incurred to date by me. Please also prepare a brief narrative report which outlines the following items.

1. Treatment rendered
2. Diagnosis
3. Prognosis
4. If applicable, an estimate of the future costs of medical care
5. Please indicate, if is true, that my injuries were caused by the automobile accident of May 1, 1998.

I will promptly remit payment for these records upon receipt of them.

Thank you in advance for your courtesy and cooperation Please feel free to contact me with any questions or concerns.

Sincerely,

Your Name

The Attorney's Duty to Reduce the Contingent Fee: In the Matter of Swartz Revisited

Douglas C. Fitzpatrick

Any personal injury attorney knows that the good cases have three components:

1. A tortfeasor with adequate liability insurance coverage or the ability to pay the claim;
2. Clear liability without issues of comparative fault or nonparties at fault;
3. Serious damages clearly caused by the tort.

The good cases can result in a substantial contingent fee without investing hundreds of hours litigating. For that matter, the prospects of earning a substantial contingent fee without even filing a lawsuit are excellent.

Ethical considerations can surface when the contingent fee becomes excessive. In fact, ethical considerations can invalidate the contingent fee agreement altogether if literal enforcement of the agreement would result in payment of an excessive fee to the attorney.

In In the Matter of Swartz, 141 Ariz. 266, 686 P2d 1236 (Supreme Court of Arizona, 1984), the client was seriously injured when hit by a car. He sustained severe multiple injuries. One leg was eventually amputated. The client, Steven Sarge, was on the job when he was injured and received worker's compensation benefits. The industrial carrier that paid the benefits had a statutory lien against the recovery in Sarge's personal injury claim.

In Sarge's tort claim against the motorist, there was no question about who was at fault. The driver was covered by two separate liability policies with limits of $50,000 and $100,000. Shortly after Sarge retained Swartz on a one-third contingent fee basis, one of the liability carriers turned over its $100,000 policy limits. About two months later, the second carrier turned over its $50,000 policy limits. The time demands on Swartz in negotiating payment of the liability insurance money were minimal. Of the $150,000 obtained by Swartz, he took $50,000 as his one-third contingent fee. The industrial carrier that paid the worker's compensation benefits received most of the remaining $100,000 by virtue of its statutory lien against the recovery. Sarge got nothing.

The Arizona Supreme court concluded that, under the circumstances, the one-third contingent fee was excessive and disciplined Swartz. The Court reasoned that, in light of the clear liability of the motorist who injured Sarge, there really was no contingency. The Court observed that there were no difficult problems in the case. In obtaining the $150,000 in liability insurance money, there were no significant demands on Swartz' time. The court also thought it was significant that Swartz didn't have to file a lawsuit. With regard to the one-third contingent fee, the Court observed that, although such fee agreements are often proper when contracted, they may turn out to be excessive:

> We hold, therefore, that if **at the conclusion of a lawyer's services**, it appears that a fee, which seemed reasonable when agreed upon, has become excessive, the attorney may not stand upon the contract; he must reduce the fee; 141 Ariz. at 273.

We learn from Swartz that, as a practical matter, the attorney may collect up to the full contingent fee contracted if (1) there is some degree of uncertainty or contingency with respect to liability; or (2) there is some other aspect of the case which renders it problematic; or (3) processing the case is labor intensive, creating significant time demands on the attorney.

Typically, the contingent fee agreement provides for a percentage lien against the recovery whether the case is settled prior to filing suit or whether the case has been litigated through a jury trial. If the attorney's fee is to be reduced, to keep it reasonable, the decision whether to compromise the fee and by what amount is left to the attorney. Untrained in the law or legal ethics, or in the absence of any provision in the fee agreement concerning the duties of the attorney under ER 1.5 or Swartz, the client would have no way to know about the duty of the attorney to reduce the fee in certain circumstances.

In the context of advertising by attorneys, ER 7.2 provides in part:

> A lawyer shall not make false or misleading communications about the lawyer or about the lawyer's services. A communication is false or misleading if it:
>
> 1. contains a material misrepresentation of fact or law or omits a fact necessary to make the statement considered as a whole not materially misleading.

ER 1.4(b) provides:

> A lawyer shall explain a matter to the extent reasonably necessary to permit the client to make informed decisions regarding the representation.

The crux of the matter is whether many attorneys are using contingent fee agreements which are significantly false or misleading. Do such agreements create the impression that the full contingent fee is to be paid to the attorney in any event? Are contingent fee agreements often misleading because they fail to disclose the ethical constraints upon the attorney which would compel a fee reduction in many situations?

There may not be any easy answers with respect to the issues raised. Dialogue within the bar concerning the ethics of drafting contingent fee agreements may be a start. If plaintiffs' attorneys are challenged to be more creative and thorough in drafting contingent fee agreements, the clients are likely to be more informed and benefit from such disclosure. The key may be to draft agreements by which the attorney's compensation is some function of the attorney's time, effort, skill and energy that have been invested into the case.

Across-the-board fixed percentage fees for all cases whether settled or tried may not comply with the letter or spirit of ER 1.5 or Swartz. Further regulation of contingent fee agreements by the Arizona Supreme Court may be the least desirable option. However, since the state's high court has already undertaken to regulate contingent fees, it might as well do so in a manner that is meaningful to both the attorney and the client. The court has found that the public is served by stringent regulation of attorney advertising. It may be that mandatory disclosures in fee agreements consistent with Swartz and ER 1.5 are the necessary next step to level the playing field between the attorney and the client.

ER 1.5 FEES

(a) A lawyer's fee shall be reasonable. The factors to be considered in determining the reasonableness of a fee include the following:

(1) the time and labor required, the novelty and difficulty of the questions involved, and the skill requisite to perform the legal service properly;

(2) the likelihood, if apparent to the client, that the acceptance of the particular employment will preclude other employment by the lawyer;

(3) the fee customarily charged in the locality for similar legal services;

(4) the amount involved and the results obtained;

(5) the time limitations imposed by the client or by the circumstances;

(6) the nature and length of the professional relationship with the client;

(7) the experience, reputation, and ability of the lawyer or lawyers performing the services; and

(8) whether the fee is fixed or contingent.

***1236** 686 P. 2d 1236

141 Ariz. 266

In the Matter of a Member of the State Bar of Arizona, John. F. SWARTZ, Respondent.

No. SB-72-3.

Supreme Court of Arizona, In Banc.

July 10, 1984.

In a disciplinary action, the Supreme Court, Feldman, J., held: (1) clearly excessive fees will constitute grounds for disciplinary action, whether the fee is fixed or contingent; (2) if at conclusion of a lawyer's services it appears that a fee, which seemed reasonable when agreed upon, has become excessive, attorney may not stand upon the contract but must reduce the fee; (3) contingent fee of $50,000 in tort action was both clearly excessive and shocking when there was no contingency, no difficult problem, and little work; (4) local administrative committee did not err by not considering results of the attorney's polygraph examination; (5) record and outcome of malpractice action against attorney was not relevant to any issue determined in bar proceedings, and thus committee's refusal to accord any weight to result of action was proper; and (6) charging excessive fee, considering prior censure, warrants suspension from practice of law for period of six months and refund of excessive portion of fee collected.

So ordered.

[141 Ariz. 268] * **1238** Stephen L. Wess, Phoenix, for State Bar.

Jack C. Cavness, Phoenix, for respondent.

FELDMAN, Justice.

A local Administrative Committee (Committee) of the State Bar of Arizona filed a complaint on September 8, 1981, alleging that John F. Swartz (respondent) violated Disciplinary Rule 2-106, Code of Professional

Responsibility, and Rule 29(b)(1) of the Rules of the Arizona Supreme Court, 17A A.R.S. (FN1), by charging a clearly excessive fee. In an amended complaint, the Committee charged that respondent's conduct also violated, *inter alia*, DR 1-102(A)(5) (conduct prejudicial to the administration of justice).

The Committee held hearings on three separate dates, ending in February, 1982. It concluded that respondent had violated DR 2-106(A) by charging and collecting a clearly excessive fee for the "total representation" of his client. Finding that respondent had attempted to maximize his fee at his client's expense, the Committee further concluded that respondent had violated DR 1-102(A)(5) by consciously and willfully taking advantage of the system for handling third party tort claims of injured workers who have sought benefits under the workmen's compensation system. A majority of the Committee recommended that respondent be suspended from practice.

Responded objected to the Committee's findings, conclusions and recommendations. The State Bar Disciplinary Board (Board) reviewed the matter and voted to accept the Committee's findings and conclusions, but modified the disciplinary action of the Committee. Respondent objected to the Board's recommendation and the matter was then filed with this court. We have jurisdiction pursuant to Rules 36(d) and 37.

FACTS

Steven Sarge was injured in a work-related accident on September 7, 1979 when the [141 Ariz. 269] ***1239** was hit by a car while setting barricades on the Black Canyon Freeway. Sarge sustained severe, multiple injuries; one leg eventually was amputated. Between September 7 and 13, while Sarge was in intensive care, respondent met with Sarge's mother and brother in the hospital room. They retained respondent to represent Sarge with respect to both a workmen's compensation claim and a personal injury claim against the responsible driver.

A.R.S. § 23-1023 permits an injured worker to follow parallel remedies. He may file a workmen's compensation claim and may, while receiving benefits, pursue a tort claim against any person (other than his employer or a co-employee) legally responsible for the injury. Such tort claims are sometimes described as "third party claims." The industrial carrier (in this case the State Compensation Fund) is given a lien against the net recovery on the third party claim for the amount of past benefits paid the injured worker. A.R.S. § 23-1023(C). Any net recovery in excess of the lien is retained by the injured worker, but is to be offset against future benefits which the worker would otherwise receive from the industrial carrier. *Id.* Thus, if there is no reasonable chance that the net tort recovery will exceed attorney's fees, costs, the workmen's compensation lien and the credit for future benefits, there is no advantage in brining the tort action, because none of the recovery would inure to the worker's benefit. An exception exists if the attorney for the worker can persuade the industrial carrier to reduce its lien, thus reducing the "nut" which the worker must meet before he may pocket any recovery. According to the evidence, one of the factors the Fund considers in determining whether to reduce its lien claim is a reduction in the amount of the fee to be charged by the attorney for the injured worker.

Sarge was seriously incapacitated and respondent appropriately established a conservatorship on November 1, 1979. On that date a written fee agreement for the tort claim was made with Sarge's mother and brother; it called for respondent to represent Sarge for a fee equal to one-third of all sums recovered.

The facts surrounding the accident were not disputed. The driver of the vehicle which struck Sarge had been intoxicated. No real defense existed and liability was clear. Punitive damages may have been recoverable. Sarge's injuries were extensive. Although a coverage issue was raised at first, it was soon abandoned, and there was no serious dispute concerning insurance coverage. In fact, the driver was covered by two separate policies, (FN2) with respective limits of $100,000 and $50,000. Aside from these two policies, there were no significant assets subject to execution or garnishment. Two weeks after respondent entered into the contingent fee agreement, one of the liability carriers offered to pay its $100,000 policy limit; approximately two months later, the second carrier offered its policy limit of $50,000. These settlements were made after minimal negotiation between respondent and representatives of the insurance carriers. It was not necessary for respondent to file the tort action and none was ever filed. Although respondent kept no time records, he testified that effecting the settlement had involved a "tremendous amount of work." A qualified expert witness called by bar counsel reviewed the files of all parties and estimated that respondent could not have spent more than twenty to thirty hours in handling all aspects of the claim.

By the time settlement was achieved it had become clear that the Fund's liability for payment of workmen's compensation benefits, and therefore its statutory lien, would soon exceed the net recovery to Sarge. In fact, at the time the settlement with the insurance carrier was consummated, the Fund's total lien was approximately $90,000. Future benefits payable, reduced to present value, were estimated at [141 Ariz. 270] ***1240** more than $150,000. The proposed settlement distribution was as follows:

Gross Settlement:	$150,000.00
Attorney's Fees (1/3):	50,000.00
Costs:	83.20
Net Proceeds:	99,917.00

As required by A.R.S. § 23-1023(C), the settlement was approved by the Fund. It was also approved by the probate court. Payment of the statutory lien in favor of the Fund consumed all but approximately $10,000 of the net of the settlement. After paying almost $90,000 of the net proceeds to the Fund in satisfaction of its lien and disbursing the fee of $50,000 to himself, respondent retained approximately $10,000 in a trust account. This sum was evidently held for payment of accruing medical expenses and the like. These "excess" funds were credited by the Fund against future benefits and constituted an offset against such benefits. From a practical standpoint, the net result of the settlement was that the Fund got $100,000, respondent received the $50,000 fee, and Sarge received nothing.

In addition to the $50,000 fee which respondent charged and collected on the recovery in the tort claim, respondent requested $1,320 and was awarded $350 in fees by the probate court for work done in the conservatorship proceedings. Respondent also charged and collected 15% of the funds which Sarge received on his workmen's compensation claim until such time as Sarge retained other counsel to represent him in connection with that claim. Respondent testified that his normal charge on workmen's compensation proceedings was 25% and that he reduced his fee to 15% because of the fee which he had received in the tort action.

Respondent and Sarge eventually had a disagreement with regard to both the compensation claim and the tort recovery; Sarge retained counsel and a malpractice action against respondent was filed in Maricopa County Superior Court. Summary judgement was granted against Sarge. The record of that action was admitted in evidence at the Committee hearing. In its findings, the Committee indicated that it had given no weight to that record, the results of the action, nor the testimony of the attorney who had represented Sarge in the malpractice action and who respondent called as a witness in the disciplinary proceedings. During respondent's case-in-chief in the disciplinary proceedings, he called a polygraph examiner to testify to the results of a polygraph test given to respondent at his request. The Committee admitted the results in connection with the issue of whether respondent had attempted to negotiate with the Fund toward compromise of its lien. (FN3) In its findings, the Committee indicated that it had not considered the polygraph results in reaching its decision.

ISSUES

Respondent contends:

1. He did not charge a clearly excessive fee and the record does not support the conclusion of the Committee that:

Respondent violated DR 2-106(A) by charging and collecting clearly an excessive fee for the total representation of his client.

2. The record does not support the Committee's findings that respondent: made absolutely no effort to obtain a reduction in the Fund's lien by compromising his attorney's fees or otherwise [with the result that] Sarge personally received nothing from the ...settlement...

Thus, respondent claims also, the Committee erred in concluding that respondent violated DR 1-102(A)(5) by "consciously and willfully" taking advantage of the system of allowing attorney's fees for third-party claims in workmen's compensation cases so as to [141 Ariz. 271] ***1241** maximize his own fees without attempting to obtain any direct monetary benefit to his client.

3. The Committee erred in failing to consider the polygraph examination results in reaching its findings of fact.

4. The Committee erred by disregarding the results of the malpractice action and the testimony of Sarge's attorney.

STANDARD OF REVIEW

[1] [2] [3] We first note the standard applicable to review of the evidence in disciplinary proceedings. Evidence of misconduct must be clear and convincing in order to support disciplinary action, but need not equal proof beyond a reasonable doubt. *In the Matter of Rubi*, 133 Ariz. 491, 652 P.2d 1014 (1982). It is our duty to make an independent determination of the ultimate facts, though the recommendations, findings of fact and conclusions of the Committee and the Board are entitled to great weight. *In the Matter of Burns*, 139 Ariz. 487 -- 679 P.2d 510, 515-516 (1984) citing *In the Matter of Lurie*, 113 Ariz. 95, 95-96, 546 P.2d 1126, 1126-27 (1976) ; *In the Matter of Rubi, supra*. Although this court is the ultimate finder of fact in disciplinary proceedings, the findings and recommendations of the Committee are especially pertinent where the credibility of a witness who testified before the Committee is at issue. *Matter of Burns, supra*.

WAS THE FEE EXCESSIVE?

DR 2-106 provides that a lawyer shall not enter into an agreement for, charge, or collect an illegal or clearly excessive fee. It provides, also, that:

B) A fee is clearly excessive when, after a review of the facts, a lawyer of ordinary prudence would be left with a definite and firm conviction that the fee is in excess of a reasonable fee.

So far as relevant to this case, the rule enumerates the following factors "to be considered as guides in determining the reasonableness of a fee":

(1) The time and labor required, the novelty and difficulty of the questions involved, and the skill requisite to perform the legal services properly.

***

***

(3) The fee customarily charged in the locality for similar legal services.

(4) The amount involved and the results obtained.

***

***

(8) Whether the fee is fixed or contingent.

DR-2-106(B)

At the Committee hearing, Bar counsel presented a qualified local attorney who gave expert testimony that the fee collected in the tort proceeding was clearly excessive. In essence, the witness testified that there was no real contingency involved in the case and that the minimal amount of work done by respondent fell far short of justifying the fee collected. The witness stated that under these facts the standard of ethical practice followed in the community would have required the respondent to greatly reduce the fee charged.

Respondent defends the propriety of the fee collected on the ground that a one-third percentage is customary for a personal injury claim in this community. He asserts that until and unless the bench and bar adopt rules regulating the amount of contingent fees, the "one-third contingent fee, which is not dependent upon work done and perhaps other considerations, is the customary fee" and may be properly charged.

We disagree, first, with the contention that appropriate regulations have not been adopted. Legal history indicates the opposite. The contingent fee was originally considered unethical and illegal as a form of champerty. *See* Note, *Lawyer's Tight Rope - Use and Abuse of Fees,* 41 Cornell L.Q. , 683, 685-86 (1956) ; Radin, *Maintenance by Champerty,* 24 Cal.L.Rev. 48 (1935); Radin, *Continent Fees in California,* 28 Cal.L.Rev. 587, 588 (1940) . It is still considered champertous and illegal in most countries, including Great Britain and the Commonwealth nations. *See* Note, *supra,* [141 Ariz. 272] ***1242** 1 Cornell L.Q. at 685 and authorities cited therein.

Whatever the view in other countries, the contingent fee was long ago recognized in the United States and is approved in nearly all, if not all, jurisdictions. Radin, *supra,* 28 Cal.L.Rev. at 589. That acceptance, however, was "grudging"; the fee was approved because it was considered a "necessary evil." Note, supra at 684-85 n. 20, quoting from Conference of Bar Association Delegates, 5 A.B.A.J. 61 (1918). To paraphrase, what was before disreputable and illegal became lawful, but not respectable. *Rooney v. Second Avenue R.R.,* 18 N.Y. 368, 373 (1858). It has been suggested that the opposition to contingent fees was chiefly based upon the fear that lawyers would speculate (Note, *supra,* at 689), the danger that lawyers with a direct pecuniary interest in a case would be tempted to manufacture or twist evidence, tamper with the process or otherwise act improperly (*id.* at 697) and the fear that lawyers would overreach because of the conflict between the profession's goal of serving the public and their own self interest. *Id.* at 705. There is also also the danger, of course, that such a fee arrangement will increase the filing of vexatious and frivolous actions, though it is certainly possible to argue that such actions may as easily be brought by lawyers who receive substantial fees on a traditional basis. Radin, *supra*, 28 Cal.L.Rev. at 589.

Whatever the dangers, it is now generally accepted that the contingent fee is proper and has substantial social utility because such arrangements are "often the only method by which a person of ordinary means may prosecute a just claim to judgment." Note, *supra*, at 689. (FN4) We believe that social utility strongly favors the contingent fee as a "poor man's door to the courthouse." Further, given present costs of litigation, we recognize that both the middle class and the wealthy may need or prefer representation on a contingent basis. Properly used, therefore, we believe that the contingent fee is a necessary method of insuring the availability of legal services. Abuses are best handled by control and regulation. In Arizona both the existence and regulation of contingent fees is recognized by our Disciplinary Rules and comments. DR 2-106(B)(8) expressly recognizes that fees may be "fixed or contingent." The Canons of Professional Ethics provide as follows:

> A contract for a contingent fee, where sanctioned by law, should be reasonable under all the circumstances of the case, including the risk and uncertainty of the compensation, but should always be subject to the supervision of the court, as to its reasonableness.
>
> Canon 13, ABA Canons of Professional Ethics, (FN5)

Thus, contrary to respondent's assertion, the contingent fee is expressly recognized in the rules and is not merely a matter of custom; *see, e.g.*, Ethical Consideration (EC) 2-20. Further, the Disciplinary Rules, adopted as binding rules of conduct, set limits for all fees, fixed and contingent. DR 2-106(B). We have recognized before that collection of clearly excessive contingent fees warrants imposition of discipline. *In the Matter of Mercer*, 126 Ariz. 274, 614 P.2d 816 (1980). The court's inherent power to prevent collection of excessive contingent fees was acknowledged in *Covert v. Randles*, 53 Ariz. 225, 230, 87 P.2d 488, 490 (1939).

[4] [5] Contrary to respondent's suggestion, DR 2-106 may be violated even though no court in this state has set any particular percentage as appropriate for [141 Ariz. 273] * 1243 contingent fees. It is no more possible to set such percentages in advance than it would be to set a single fixed fee for all divorce cases or all real estate litigation. We hold, therefore, that contingent fees are subject to regulation by this court. Excessive fees should not be charged

(ABA Canons of Professional Ethics, Canon 12) and "clearly excessive fees" will constitute grounds for disciplinary action, whether the fee is fixed or contingent. DR 2-106.

[6] [7] Respondent is correct in contending that the one-third contingent fee initially agreed upon was within customary limits for the type of case and was not excessive. We do not believe, however, that recognition of the propriety of the initial fee arrangement gives the lawyer carte blanche to charge the agreed percentage regardless of the circumstances which eventually develop. Either a fixed or contingent fee, proper when contracted for, may later turn out to be excessive. Radin, *supra*, 28 Cal.L.Rev. at 591. We realize that business contracts may be enforced between those in equal bargaining capacities, even though they turn out to be unfair, inequitable or harsh. *Goodman v. Newzona Invest. Co*, 101 Ariz. 470, 473-474, 421 P.2d 318, 321-322 (1966). However, a fee agreement between lawyer and client is not an ordinary business contract. The profession has both an obligation of public service and duties to clients which transcend ordinary business relationships and prohibit the lawyer from taking advantage of the client. Thus, in fixing and collecting fees the profession must remember that it is "a branch of the administration of justice and and not a mere money getting trade." ABA Canons of Professional Ethics, Canon 12. We hold, therefore, that if at the conclusion of a lawyer's services it appears that a fee, which seemed reasonable when agreed upon, has become excessive, the attorney may not stand upon the contract; he must reduce the fee. What is reasonable and within permissible limits will be determined by the circumstances, including the factors listed in DR 2-106.

[8] In the case at bench, we believe that at the time of settlement it was obvious that the agreed fee was unreasonable and clearly excessive. We recognize that a lawyer working on a contingent fee basis may receive a large fee without that fee being excessive. The fee may be much larger than that which the attorney would have received if he had made no agreement and sued for the reasonable value of his services. Radin, supra, 28 Cal.L.Rev. at 592. It may be much larger than that attorney or others in the community would have charged had they been retained and paid on a time basis. Such disparity is inherent in the nature of a contingent fee and is, therefore, one of the circumstances to be considered under DR 2-106(B)(8). Nevertheless, also inherent in the nature of the contingent fee is the concept that the share of the recovery to be paid the lawyer as a contingent fee is properly the product of a number of factors, including: 1) the degree of uncertainty or contingency with respect to liability, amount of damages which may be recovered, or the funds available from which to collect any judgment; 2) the difficulty of the case and the skill required to handle it; 3) the time expended in pursuing it; and, 4) the results obtained. In the case at bench there was no contingency or uncertainty as to liability, and it was apparent that the damages would be substantial but

recovery limited to the relatively small amount or insurance available. The limits of the insurance policies available were known almost immediately. There was nothing novel or difficult about the case and it was not even necessary to file a legal action. At the most, only thirty hours of time were expended on the case. There was, in short, no contingency, no difficult problem and little work. There was also no result for the client. Under these circumstances, we agree with the Bar's expert that a fee of $50,000 is both clearly excessive and shocking. Had respondent not deducted the fee but attempted to recover it from Sarge by legal action, it would have been the "duty" of this court "to deny a recovery" on the ground that the fee was out of proportion to the services [141 Ariz. 274] ***1244** rendered. *Covert v. Randles, supra.* In dealing with his client, respondent may not be allowed to obtain by self-help what he could not have properly obtained in a court of law. When it became evident that the fee agreed upon was excessive, it became respondent's duty to reduce the agreed fee so that he would charge and collect no more than was reasonable.

Respondent argues, however, that the fee can not be considered excessive because it was approved by both the State Compensation Fund and the Probate Court. We disagree. The evidence showed that such "approvals" are made on a pro forma basis with no real inquiry into the factors that determine whether the fee is reasonable. An arrangement calling for a one-third contingent fee seems reasonable on its face, and may well have been approved, according to the testimony, without real inquiry.

[9] Respondent argues, also, that the amount of the fee had no effect on his client because the client would have recovered nothing even if the fee had been smaller. Respondent contends that reduction of the fee would only have resulted in a greater recovery by the Fund, which was not his client and to which, the argument continues, he had no duty. Assuming, *arguendo*, that all this is true (see *post*, p. 1244), we believe that respondent misapprehends his obligation.The issue is not one of tort duty to the Fund, but a question of the duty which respondent owes to the system of justice. Even if respondent owed no legal duty to the Fund, he owed his client, the profession and the judicial system an ethical obligation of charging no more than was reasonable. The profession's ethical requirements do not permit an attorney to extract unreasonable fees simply because those who must bear the ultimate loss are not in a lawyer/client relationship with the attorney. The axiom that a lawyer's duty is owed to his client does not support the corollary that all others are fair game.

We hold, therefore, the respondent did collect a clearly excessive fee in violation of DR 2-106(A). The Committee's findings and conclusions on this issue are approved and adopted.

ATTORNEYS' CONTINGENT FEES LIMITS INITIATIVE STATUTE

Limits fees which plaintiffs' attorneys may collect if payment contingent on plaintiffs' recovery of compensation in personal injury, wrongful death, other tort cases. Requires demand against defendants for compensation with supporting information. Allows defendants to respond with early settlement offer with supporting information. If accepted, plaintiffs' attorneys may not collect contingent fees exceeding 15% of defendants' offer. If not accepted, they may collect fees above 15% only on part of recovery in excess of defendants' early settlement offer.

SECTION ONE. This Act shall be known as the "Lawyer Contingent Fee Limitation Act."

SECTION TWO. The People of the State of California declare:

(a) The contingent-fee arrangements lawyers typically negotiate with claimants, most of whom are inexperienced and unsophisticated purchasers of legal services, often require claimants to pay their lawyers too much for handling tort claims that a defendant has offered to settle.

(b) These excessive fees harm claimants by depriving them of compensation they deserve.

(c) The excessive fees also discourage early settlement of tort claims, forcing injured people to suffer long delays in receiving compensation and clogging the courts with lawsuits that should not have to be filed.

(d) Imposing a cap on the fees lawyers can charge for handling tort claims that a defendant has offered to settle quickly would:

(1) Prevent lawyers from taking an unreasonable portion of the compensation offered or awarded to an injured person.

(2) Encourage defendants to settle claims quickly.

(3) Enable injured people to be compensated more promptly.

(4) Relieve some of the present burden placed on the courts, reducing costs for taxpayers, and enabling other legal disputes to be resolved more quickly.

SECTION THREE: Sections 6146.1, 6146.2, 6146.3, 6146.4, 6146.5, and 6146.6 of Article 8.5 of Chapter 4 of Division 3 of the Business and Professions Code are added as follows:

6146.1 [CONTINGENT-FEE LIMITATIONS] (a) An attorney who represents a claimant who has accepted an early settlement offer shall not collect a contingent fee that is greater than 15% of the amount of the early settlement offer.

(b) An attorney who represents a claimant who has rejected or failed to accept an early settlement offer shall not collect a contingent fee that is greater than 15% of the amount of the early settlement offer plus such percentage of the amount recovered in excess of the early settlement offer as was agreed to by the claimant and the attorney.

(c) A claimant's attorney who has failed to make a demand for compensation pursuant to Section 6146.2 or who has omitted from such demand information required under Section 6146.2 of a material nature which the attorney had in his or her possession or which was readily available to him or her, shall not collect a contingent fee greater than 15% of the amount recovered.

(d) A claimant's attorney who has failed to provide his or her client a true and complete copy of an early settlement offer received by the attorney, as required under subdivision (c) of Section 6146.3, shall not collect a contingent fee greater than 15% of the amount recovered.

(e) Reasonable costs and expenses incurred by an attorney up to that time of receipt of an early settlement offer shall be deducted from that settlement offer for purposes of calculating the maximum permissible fee under subdivisions (a) and (b).

(f) An attorney shall disclose, plainly and in writing, to claimants whom the attorney proposes to represent on a contingent-fee basis, (1) the fee limitations imposed by this section and (2) the fact that such limitations are maximum limits and that the attorney and claimant may negotiate a lower fee. The attorney shall also provide to each such claimant a copy of this act.

(g) The fee limitations imposed by this section may not be waived.

(h) The provisions of this section apply to all attorneys practicing in California, including attorneys prosecuting claims filed in federal court, to the maximum extent permitted by federal law.

6146.2 [CLAIMANT'S DEMAND FOR COMPENSATION] (a) An attorney representing a claimant on a contingent-fee basis shall send a demand for compensation by certified mail to each allegedly responsible party. In the event that multiple allegedly responsible parties are known to the attorney, a demand shall be sent on the same date to each party. The demand shall specify the amount of compensation sought and shall set forth the material facts, documentary evidence, and other information relevant to the demand, including:

(1) The name and address of the claimant or of the person on whose behalf the claim is being made.

(2) A brief description of how the injury or loss occurred.

(3) The names and, if known, the addresses and telephone numbers of all known witnesses to the injury or loss.

(4) Copies of photographs in the claimant's possession which relate to the injury or loss.

(5) The basis for claiming that the party to whom the demand is addressed is responsible or partially responsible for the injury or loss.

(6) A description of the nature of the injury or loss, including the dates and nature of the care or services provided, and the names and addresses of all physicians and other health-care providers that provided medical care or services to the claimant or injured party.

(7) Medical records relating to the injury, including those involving a prior injury or pre-existing medical condition which would be discoverable by the allegedly responsible party during the course of litigation or, in lieu thereof, executed releases authorizing the allegedly responsible party to obtain such records directly from those health-care providers who provided treatment to the claimant.

(8) Documentation of any medical expenses, lost wages, personal losses, and other economic and non-economic losses suffered as a consequence of the injury or loss.

(b) The attorney shall mail copies of each demand to the claimant and to each and every allegedly responsible party.

(c) A claimant's attorney who learns of an additional allegedly responsible party after making a demand for compensation under subdivision (a) shall send a demand of compensation to the newly discovered allegedly responsible party and simultaneously mail a copy of such demand to each of the other allegedly responsible parties and to the claimant.

(d) In the event that a claimant's attorney learns of an additional allegedly responsible party more than 90 days after making a demand for compensation under subdivision (a), the attorney shall not be required to send a demand to that party nor shall the fee limitations imposed under subdivisions (a) and (b) of Section 6146.1 apply with regard to any amount recovered from that party, excepted as next provided. An attorney who fails as a result of a breach of the standard of care to learn of an additional allegedly responsible party within 90 days of sending a demand for compensation to another allegedly responsible party shall not collect a fee in excess of that allowed under subdivisions (a) and (b) of Section 6146.1 with respect to any amount recovered from such additional allegedly responsible party.

6146.3 [EARLY SETTLEMENT OFFER] (a) An offer by an allegedly responsible party to settle a claim shall constitute an early settlement offer if the allegedly responsible party:

(1) makes the settlement offer within 60 days of receipt of a demand for compensation;

(2) communicates the offer in writing and by certified mail to the claimant's attorney;

(3) leaves the offer open for acceptance for a minimum of 30 days from the date of its receipt by the claimant's attorney; and

(4) includes with the offer material information and documentary evidence in its possession relating to the alleged injury or loss upon which the allegedly responsible party relied in making the settlement offer, including:

(A) Copies of photographs which relate to the injury or loss.

(B) The basis for claiming, if it is so claimed, that the allegedly responsible party is not responsible, or is less responsible than is alleged by the claimant, for the alleged injury or loss.

(C) Information regarding injuries or losses suffered by the claimant.

(b) An allegedly responsible party may amend or issue an additional early settlement offer during the 60-day period set for in subdivision (a). An amended or additional early settlement offer shall be subject to the requirements set forth in subdivision (a).

(c) A settlement offer that is made to a claimant prior to receipt of a demand for compensation, and which conforms to the requirements of subdivision (a) shall be deemed an early settlement offer and shall have the same effect as if it were a response to a demand for compensation.

(d) An allegedly responsible party is under no obligation to issue a response to a demand for compensation. The fact that a demand for compensation was or was not made, the fact that an early settlement offer was or was not made, and the amount of any demand or settlement offer made are inadmissible pursuant to Section 1152 of the Evidence Code.

(e) An attorney who receives an early settlement offer shall provide a true and complete copy of such offer to his or her client.

6146.4 [ENFORCEMENT] A claimant who is charged a contingent fee that is higher than that authorized under Section 6146.1, except as provided under subdivision (d) of Section 6146.2, may maintain an action against that attorney. Such claimant is entitled to recover from such attorney three times the amount overcharged or $10,000, whichever is greater.

6146.5 [FIDUCIARY RELATIONSHIP] A fiduciary relationship applies with respect to any fee agreement between an attorney and a claimant.

6146.6 [DEFINITIONS] For purposes of Section 6146.1 through 6146.5, the following terms have the following meanings:

(1) "Allegedly responsible party" means a person, partnership, or corporation alleged by a claimant to be responsible for at lease some portion of an injury or loss alleged by that claimant.

(2) "Amount recovered" means the total compensation, including the reasonable value of non-monetary compensation, that an attorney has obtained on behalf of a claimant through settlement, arbitration, or judgment, minus the reasonable costs and expenses incurred by the attorney in prosecuting or settling the claim.

(3) "Claimant" means any natural person or persons seeking compensation in connection with a tort claim including, but not limited to, a claim for personal injury or wrongful death. However, a claimant does not include any person or persons seeking compensation in connection with a claim covered by Section 6146, a claim for workers' compensation benefits, or a case in which a court has certified the existence of a class action pursuant to state or federal law.

(4) "Contingent fee" means compensation, however calculated, that is payable only if an amount is recovered.

(5) “Early Settlement offer" means a settlement offer made in accordance with Section 6146.3.

SECTION FOUR. (a) Except as provided in subdivision (b) of this section, the provisions of this initiative shall not be amended except by a statute that becomes effective only when approved by the electorate.

(b) The provisions of this initiative may be amended only to further its purposes, by a statute passed in each house of the Legislature by roll call vote entered in the journal, two-thirds of the membership of each house concurring. In any judicial action with respect to such amendment, the court shall exercise its independent judgment and shall determine whether the amendment is supported by findings clearly and convincingly establishing that the amendment furthers the initiative's purposes.

SECTION FIVE. If any provision of this act or application thereof to any person or circumstance is held invalid, that invalidity shall not affect other provisions or applications of the act which can be given effect without the invalid provision or application, and to this end the provisions of the act are severable.

APPENDIX

SAMPLE DEMAND LETTERS

Your settlement proposal ("demand letter") represents weeks or months of record keeping, journaling, investigation, research, and analysis concerning your claim. If your claim is to settle for a reasonable amount, it's because your letter is well-reasoned, detailed, and supported by the appropriate back up documentation.

Every settlement proposal will include a discussion of both liability or allocation of fault and damages. If liability is not at issue, your letter will simply say so. The demand will conclude with a proposal to settle for a sum certain which allows room for negotiation.

Supporting documentation should include witness statements, accident reports, medical bills, medical records, photographs, and any other relevant records. Time and space do not permit inclusion of back up documentation for each of the sample demand letters included here.

The following settlement proposals reflect a variety of fact patterns and damages scenarios, each of which is unique. Paraphrase those portions of the letters which are applicable to your situation.

Date

State Farm Insurance
Attention: Jane Doe
P O Box 3690
Flagstaff, AZ 86003-3690

Chubb Group of Insurance Companies
Attention: Nancy Roe
Two Embarcadero Center, Suite 1500
San Francisco, CA 94111

RE: Claimant -- Carrie Neal
Date of Loss -- May 18, 2000

Chubb Claim #1234
Chubb Insured – Martin Neal

State Farm Claim #5678
State Farm Insured – Mark Zack

Dear Ms. Doe and Ms. Roe:

You will recall that I represent Carrie Neal. I am writing in connection with the above matters and in the hope that my client's claims will be settled.

LIABILITY/ALLOCATION OF FAULT

This accident occurred on May 18, 2000, at about 10:37 a.m. Mr. Zack was proceeding northbound in the inner left-hand lane of Interstate 17 in the vicinity of Mile Post 292 near McGuireville. He was driving a rented late model Jeep Cherokee. The weather was clear and the road was dry. Interstate 17 has two northbound lanes and two southbound lanes separated by a large median.

My client, Carrie Neal, was a passenger in the front seat of a 1996 Ford Explorer driven by her husband, Martin Neal. The Neals were returning to their home in Sedona after a brief visit to Camp Verde. Mr. Neal was driving in the right-hand or outer lane of traffic just before the accident. He was driving side by side with Mr. Zack when Mr. Zack came upon a slower moving vehicle also in the inner left-hand lane. Mr. Zack was forced to slow down slightly because of the slower moving vehicle in front of him. As Mr. Zack slowed, the Neal vehicle began to move ahead of the Zack vehicle. Although Mr. Neal was in the process of passing the Zack vehicle when the accident occurred, it was not because he accelerated. He made what was a slow pass because Zack was forced to decelerate as a result of the vehicle in front of him. Upon slowing, Mr. Zack made a sudden shift into the Neals' lane. Anticipating an impact, my client shouted "My God! He's coming into our lane!" The Neals' vehicle then skidded out of control across the two lanes of traffic, rolled and came to rest on its side.

I am enclosing a copy of the accident report from the Department of Public Safety and Mr. Neal's statement taken by Jane Doe. Also enclosed is a narrative report which summarizes the statement given by Ron Rockwell who was driving northbound on I-17 about 100 yards behind the Neal and Zack vehicles.

The evidence supports a finding that Mr. Zack made an unsafe lane change which forced Mr. Neal to take evasive action and, ultimately, lose control of his vehicle. Mr. Zack was clearly not safely ahead or behind the Neals' vehicle when he attempted to move into their lane. Mr. Zack admitted to the investigating DPS officer that the Neals were in his blind spot when he started to move right into their lane. All he had to do was look to his right and he would have seen the Neals. He failed to do so. Mr. Zack's conduct was both negligent and negligent per se. In attempting to move into the right hand lane of traffic without being safely clear of the Neals' vehicle, he violated ARS sec. 28-723(1).

It appears that Mr. Zack had no reason to be driving in the left hand lane. ARS sec. 28-721(A) requires persons to drive on the right side of the road except under certain narrow exceptions none of which are applicable to the facts before us. If Mr. Zack had been driving in the right hand lane, the accident would not have occurred.

In reviewing the statement of Don Rockwell, it appears there is conflicting evidence with respect to Mr. Neal's speed. Mr. Rockwell thought that Mr. Neal was exceeding the posted speed limit by several miles per hour. Mr. Neal estimated his speed at 75 mph immediately before the accident. After investigating the accident, the DPS officer also estimated Mr. Neal's speed at 75 mph. The posted speed limit is 75 mph.

In light of the fact that Mr. Rockwell is an independent witness, there exists some prospect that a jury would conclude that Mr. Neal did violate the posted speed limit just before the accident occurred. However, it's unlikely that Mr. Neal's alleged speeding would be found to be the cause of the accident. The primary cause of the accident was Mark Zack's failure to look where he was going in negotiating the lane change. As a practical matter, a jury is not likely to find Mr. Neal primarily at fault for the accident. Who does not violate the speeding laws, by a few miles per hour, on a regular basis?

I recognize that Mrs. Neal was not seat belted at the time of the accident. This is a non-issue in light of the speed of the vehicle and the nature of the crash. We will present expert testimony, if we need to, that serious injuries to the upper extremities are likely in high-speed rollover collisions without regard to seat belt use or non-use. The testimony would be that the upper extremities tend to flop around within the vehicle, resulting in serious injuries. It is equally true that while a lap belt with shoulder harness protects the lumbar spine and upper torso, it results in additional loading upon and injury to the cervical spine.

In light of the foregoing and for settlement purposes only, I propose that fault be allocated as follows for Carrie Neal's damages: seventy-five percent (75%) to Mark Zack and twenty-five percent (25%) to Martin Neal. If litigation is necessary with the resulting finger pointing between Messrs. Neal and Zack as to fault issues, that will only engender greater sympathy for Carrie Neal who was clearly blameless for this tragic accident.

DAMAGES

At the scene of the accident, Mrs. Neal managed to crawl out of the Ford Explorer, notwithstanding her debilitating injuries. She was transported to the Verde Valley Medical Center by ambulance.

My client's injuries were diagnosed as follows:

1. left tibia fracture
2. right distal radius (wrist) fracture
3. severe abrasions to the right knee.

Emergency surgery performed by orthopedist Dr. Jack Warren included the following:

1. He placed a titanium rod ("nail") in my client's left tibia
2. He performed a closed reduction and placement of an EBI external fixator in my client's right upper extremity
3. He thoroughly irrigated and debrided the deep abrasions to Mrs. Neal's right knee and repaired the skin. Within a day or two after the emergency surgery, Mrs. Neal required a blood transfusion.

Life has been an uphill battle for my client since the accident. In a June 28 follow up visit with Dr. Warren, he removed brown glass from her lower leg. On July 12, he removed the external fixator from Mrs. Neal's right upper extremity. My client was not prepared for the extreme pain that resulted from the sudden removal of support from her right arm. This extreme discomfort lasted for several weeks. In another follow up visit with Dr. Warren on August 9, more glass was removed from my client's left leg.

Ever since the surgery on May 18, 2000, Mrs. Neal experienced discomfort, especially when walking, as a result of the surgical hardware installed by Dr. Warren. She was forced to use a walker and orthopedic boot for two and a half months after the initial surgery. (My client would have to rely on the walker and special boot again for six plus weeks after the surgery of March 27, 2001 to remove the titanium rod.) She sought a second opinion and follow up care from Dr. Timothy Bowles on August 16 with regard to removal of the hardware. On September 7, my client was again placed under a general anesthetic in connection with Dr. Bowles' removal of four interlocking screws from her left leg. In the course of this procedure, yet another glass fragment (4-mm X 5-mm) was removed from Mrs. Neal's left leg.

The last surgery occurred on March 27, 2001. For the third time, Dr. Warren placed Mrs. Neal under a general anesthetic in connection with the removal of the titanium rod from her leg. This surgery set my client back to the point that she was, again, in much pain and requiring a walker to ambulate. This final round of recovery is to last six to eight weeks.

In addition to the symptoms associated with my client's broken right wrist and left leg, she developed shoulder symptoms from using the walker in attempting to ambulate with her fractured wrist. Records from Donna Sgariglia DC are enclosed which relate to Dr. Sgariglia's treatment of the shoulder symptoms.

Prior to the accident, Mrs. Neal had been a positive upbeat individual who looked for the best in every situation, no matter what the challenge. The physical and emotional pain in the last year has brought Carrie Neal to the depths of despair. Although my client is determined that she will recover from her injuries and the events of this last year, you need to know some of the details that would be considered by a jury in assessing damages.

Dealing with the physical and emotional pain has resulted in severe sleep disturbance that continues. Mrs. Neal has had to work through anger, fatigue, depression and a sense of hopelessness. Last summer, my client and her husband had purchased a home in Sedona. What was to be a joyous and memorable time of excitement moving into the new home became a chore and ordeal, as they had to move only three weeks after the accident. The anticipation of a visit by Mrs. Neal with her grown children and her new sixteen-pound grandson was overshadowed by concern that she wouldn't be able to hold the precious addition to the family because of her broken wrist.

Mrs. Neal and her husband have been married for 37 years. Accident-related pain caused, in part, by Mr. Neal has resulted in an emotional separation between the Neals. My client does not like to consider the possibility that her marriage may be in jeopardy. Because of Mrs. Neal's convalescence, there have been many physical demands that have fallen upon her husband, rendering him short-tempered and angry. There has been more discord in the marriage, since the accident, than in the Neals' previous 36 years of marriage combined. In short, the events of this last year have resulted in the most difficult period of life ever experienced by my client.

Mrs. Neal's dramatic scars will always serve as a reminder of the accident. Her right knee and left leg are badly scarred, as are her right wrist and arm. My client has explored the feasibility and cost of cosmetic surgery to repair these damages. She has been told that the prospects of a positive result are not good. Apparently, skin on the leg does not respond to plastic surgery as does skin on the face.

My client has experienced numbness in her foot since the accident. She has come to learn that this will be a permanent symptom. She has also lost flexibility in her wrist, which is unlikely to return. She experiences pain and swelling in her wrist when she uses it. The prospect of debilitating arthritis in the joints impacted by the trauma of the accident is another source of concern for Mrs. Neal.

There have been economic losses resulting from the accident. Mrs. Neal was looking forward to setting up a practice as a psychotherapist. She is licensed in Kentucky as a clinical social worker and was in the process of getting licensed in Arizona. I have a package of materials that was mailed to my client from the Board of Behavioral Health Examiners, postmarked March

3, 2000, which provides further evidence of my client's intent to set up a practice in Sedona. Because of the accident and resulting pain, confusion, and chaos in my client's life for the last year, these plans had to be put on hold. My client is entitled to recover the income she would have earned during the year she was in recovery.

Mrs. Neal has an interest in the economic losses suffered by her husband as a result of the accident. Mr. Neal is a forensic and structural engineer, licensed as such in nine states. He is also a licensed land surveyor. Mr. Neal had just set up a practice in Sedona when the accident occurred. Evidence of such intent is demonstrated by a Yellow Pages listing for the year 2000 which Mr. Neal purchased in February. He is listed in the sections for Forensic Engineers and Structural Engineers. Mr. Neal has the ability to earn in excess of $100,000 when he is working full time. The demands on Mr. Neal, as a result of the accident, frustrated his plans to build a profitable practice as an engineer.

We have not hired an economist to quantify the income loss sustained by Mrs. Neal as a result of the accident. For the purpose of settlement, we would just as soon assign a reasonable and conservative figure about which I would hope there could be no serious disagreement. Such estimate is $30,000.

Other economic losses include a claim for the loss of household services. Again, a reasonable estimate in light of the seriousness of my client's impairment for the greater part of a year is $10,000.

In weighing my client's claims, please consider her appearance, personality and demeanor. Carrie Neal is an attractive and personable woman who would make a sympathetic witness on her own behalf. She has an amazing determination to get better, put these problems behind her and get on with living life to the fullest. To her credit, I have no doubt that she will do this. In the meantime, she is entitled to be reasonably compensated for her losses caused by your insureds.

To recap the hard numbers, we claim the following damages:

Medical bills	$48,678
Lost income	$30,000
Loss of household services	$10,000

The reasonable verdict potential for my client's claim, in light of all the foregoing, is $300,000 to $350,000. I have Mrs. Neal's authorization to settle for $290,000.

This settlement package is tendered pursuant to Rule 408, Arizona Rules of Evidence.

Yours truly,

XYZ

Enclosure
c: Carrie Neal

Date

Mr. John Jones
This Town Insurance Group
P O Box 00
Anytown, USA

RE: Insured -- Omer Doe
Claim #0000
Date of Loss --
Claimants -- Vernon Smith

Dear Mr. Jones:

I am writing with respect to the claim of Vernon Smith and with the expectation that it can be settled.

The accident occurred on August 21, 1999, in Rockfield. Mr. Smith was a passenger in a vehicle driven by Larry Brown. I represent Mr. Brown in a companion claim. Mr. Smith's accident-related symptoms are substantially relieved and he is medically stable. Because Mr. Brown continues to treat and the full extent of his accident-related injuries are not yet known, it would be premature to settle his claim.

My clients were in a relatively small Chevrolet Cavalier northbound on Badger Hill Road, waiting for traffic to clear before making a left hand turn into a parking lot. Mr. Brown had his left hand turn signal on. They were hit from the rear by Mr. Doe who was driving a 3/4 ton pick up truck. Mr. Doe's speed at the moment of impact was estimated by the investigating officer to be 45 mph. Your insured, who left about 90 feet of skid marks, told the sheriff's deputy that he didn't recall how fast he was going. The posted speed limit is 35 mph. Mr. Doe apologized to my clients at the scene for causing the accident.

Mr. Doe was cited for a violation of ARS sec. 28-701, failing to keep his vehicle under control. The evidence supports our contention that your insured exceeded the posted speed limit. I will assume, for the purpose of settlement negotiations, that liability is not an issue and that fault for the accident rests solely with Mr. Doe. If you have contrary evidence, please bring it to my attention and I will reassess my position with respect to liability.

The vehicle occupied by my clients sustained substantial damage. The rear bumper and trunk were smashed inward. The property damage claim has been resolved.

Mr. Smith was a passenger in the front seat by the window. He heard the squeal of Mr. Doe's tires just seconds before impact. He was seat belted. When he heard your insured closing in at an excessive rate of speed, he turned to his left to look out of the rear window. Mr. Smith's upper torso and neck were fully rotated at the moment of impact. In light of the severity of the rear-end impact from a speeding 3/4 ton pick up truck into my client whose spine was fully rotated, there should be no doubt that Mr. Smith was seriously injured. The seat belt worn by my client compounded the trauma to his cervical spine.

The onset of symptoms was not immediate. Mr. Smith sustained bruising on his chest and upper torso from the seat belts. Within hours after the accident, my client began to experience neck pain, lower back pain, frequent headaches, difficulty concentrating, and other symptoms more specifically detailed in the medical records.

I trust that you will review the medical records which outline Mr. Smith's course of treatment. Although he sought help from Dr. George for approximately five months after the accident, he didn't get much relief. He had come to wonder whether anyone would be able to help him. After he was told by Dr. George that there was nothing more she could do for him, Mr. Smith tried to accept the fact that his continuing symptoms were something he would have to live with on a long term or permanent basis. Fortunately, Dr. Michael Hamner was able to treat my client with results. Thanks to Dr. Hamner, Mr. Smith is almost back to normal and medically stable.

My client's medical bills include the following:

Marie George DC	$ 4,697
Michael F. Hamner DC	7,780
Gary Longmont, MSc.	95
Total:	$12,572

Mr. Smith has been employed in a landscaping business owned by his brother. He had been a hands-on supervisor, working side by side with his subordinates. After the accident, he was not able to participate in the physical labor but continued to work in a supervisory capacity. He missed considerable time from work to seek treatment. Apparently because of the good graces of his brother, there has been no wage loss of consequence.

To sum up, Mr. Smith was seriously injured in the accident of August 21, 1999. He experienced debilitating symptoms from that date and through his treatment with Dr. Hamner which was concluded earlier this month. For one and a half years, the quality of Mr. Smith's life has been impaired as a result of the frequent headaches, neck pain, and lower back pain. My client is a clean cut young man who would make a credible and sympathetic witness on his own behalf in front of a jury.

Mr. Smith's claim has a verdict potential of $25,000 to $35,000. In the interest of avoiding the uncertainty and expense of litigation, I have my client's authority to settle for $30,000.

Please contact me at your earliest convenience if you have any questions and to bring this matter to conclusion.

Yours truly,

XYZ

Date

Ms. Janice Stone
Anytown Insurance
P O Box 0000
Anytown, USA

RE: CLAIM #
DATE OF LOSS:
SF INSURED: ROBERT M. JONES
CLAIMANT: DONALD DOE

Dear Ms. Stone:

I am writing to settle Donald Doe's claim.

The accident occurred on August 22, 2000, in Condon, Wyoming at about 8:15 a.m. The weather was clear and dry and my client was on his way to work. He was driving a 1996 Ford F150 four wheel drive. Donald was seat-belted with a lap belt and shoulder harness.

My client was at a complete stop when hit from the rear by Mr. Jones. The impact from your insured knocked Donald's vehicle into a Blazer in front of him. I understand that one or more of the occupants of the Blazer were injured by the impact. Mr. Jones was driving a smaller vehicle the engine, radiator and front bumper of which were severely damaged. Donald describes the front end of your insured's vehicle as having been "taken out." The cost to repair my client's pick up truck was approximately $2000.

Mr. Jones failed to control his vehicle to avoid the impact with Donald's pick up truck. It also appears that fault for the accident rests solely with your insured. If you have evidence to suggest that persons other than Mr. Jones are responsible for my client's damages, please bring it to my attention and I'll reconsider my assumption that Mr. Jones is 100% at fault.

At the time of accident, Donald was employed by Decora Metalworks ("Decora"). The metalworking business was a trade which had been pursued by my client's father and grandfather. Donald had planned to make a career out of the metalworking business himself until he was injured in this accident.

Donald had been earning $11/hour and working about 50 hours a week. His take home pay was approximately $430 a week. Donald was unable to work at all for two weeks after the accident (8/22-9/5). Upon returning to work, Donald was able to handle light duty only and then for about 1/3 of his normal work week. He tried to be productive by cleaning, mowing lawns, and performing whatever other tasks his employer could find to keep him busy. Soon it became apparent that, because of the physical limitations caused by accident-related symptoms, he would have to quit. Donald worked light duty from September 5 until he left Wyoming to relocate in California on October 15.

A recap which reflects Donald's lost wages in Wyoming is as follows:

8/22 - 9/5	two weeks with no work (at $430/wk)	$ 860
9/6 - 10/15	six weeks at one third capacity ("light duty")	
	six weeks net wages at $430/wk	
	should have been	2,580
	six weeks earning at 1/3 capacity was	860
	net loss for 9/6 - 10/15	$ 1,720
Total		**$ 2,580**

When Donald moved to California, he was able to go to work for his mother who owns a car wash. He has been earning $8/hour for 40 hours per week. It is obvious that the economic losses associated with the accident continued for Donald after his change of domicile to California.

Copies of my client's medical records are provided. For the first few days after the accident, Donald's feet would go numb. For months after the accident and until he was through treating with James Williams, he suffered from numbness and sharp pains in his thighs and buttocks. As he convalesced, Donald experienced muscle spasms, anxiety, irritability, and loss of sleep. The symptoms and course of treatment are detailed in the medical records.

Donald was forced to rely on pain pills and muscle relaxers to survive his accident related symptoms. Even during the weeks he worked light duty for Decora, his back felt like it was "on fire" at the end of the work day.

Donald had been an active and athletic young man prior to the accident. Recreational activities including four wheeling, hiking, and hunting had to be curtailed during his convalescence. The accident took place three days before a hunting trip in eastern Wyoming for which Donald had been saving all summer. He was unable to go on the trip because of his injuries. As of November 16, 2000, when I first met Donald, he still could not hike with his dog or walk any distance on a flat surface without pain.

After the accident and because of the related financial setbacks, Donald's roommate in Wyoming had to pay all of the rent. His financial and moral indebtedness to his roommate are damages caused by the accident.

The medical bills of $1,269.86 are relatively minor compared to all that Donald's been through and his other losses. As we discussed, Donald's carrier, Allstate, has a lien against any recovery he may receive from Anytown Insurance. I have a call in to Allstate to request a compromise of its lien for med pay benefits paid by it. I will, in any case, see that the lien is satisfied.

Prior to the accident, Donald had had no health problems involving his neck, back, or spine. To the contrary, he had been an active athletic young man. Life did not return to normal until Donald was through with the physical therapy which went from December 14, 2000, to March 13, 2001. For more than six months, Donald endured the symptoms of his accident-caused injuries.

In putting a value on my client's losses and the reasonable settlement value of his claim, I would be remiss if I didn't mention that this is an attractive, personable and clean cut young man who would make a sympathetic witness on his own behalf.

After discussing Donald's options with him, I have his authority to settle for $15,000. Please contact me at your earliest convenience to dispose of this matter.

Thank you.

Yours truly,

XYZ

Date

Mr. Insurance Adjuster
Anytown Insurance Group
P O Box 1234
Anytown, OH 45214

RE: *Claimant --* *John Doe*
Insured -- *Jane Brown*
Claim No. -- *1234567*

Dear Mr. Adjuster:

I am writing in an effort to settle the above-captioned claim.

You have reviewed the accident report and have a basic understanding of the dynamics of the accident. My client, John Doe, was a passenger in a van that collided with your insured. The owner and operator of the van was John Smith. The van did not have seat belts or my client would have been wearing them as he is in the habit of wearing seat belts. Your insured failed to yield the right of way when she pulled in front of Mr. Smith's van while apparently attempting to make a left-hand turn onto Main Street. I understand that the sun was setting behind Mr. Smith's van and that your insured may have been temporarily blinded when she attempted to negotiate her turn.

The posted speed limit was 50 miles per hour at the scene of the accident. The investigating officer reported that Mr. Smith was doing the speed limit immediately prior to impact. My client and Mr. Green, the other passenger, estimated Mr. Smith's speed to be significantly lower than 50 mph. In any case, it would appear that Mr. Smith was faultless with respect to the accident. It is reasonable to assume that Ms. Brown was one hundred percent (100%) at fault.

At the time of the accident, Mr. Doe was employed by Quality Builders as a carpenter. He was earning $10 per hour and working forty-hour weeks (eight-hour days). He missed August 3 and August 4 because of accident-related symptoms. Half way through the day on August 10 accident-related symptoms flared up making it impossible for Mr. Doe to continue work. He then missed August 11 and August 12 while employed by Quality

Builders. We total his lost wages while working for Quality Builders to be four and one-half days, or $360 in gross wages. A letter from Mr. Stone at Quality Builders is enclosed to substantiate Mr. Doe's employment and rate of pay. If you need further details, feel free to contact Mr. Stone directly. Your Authorization for Release of Wage Information form, signed by Mr. Doe, is enclosed.

My client had the opportunity to go to work for another framing contractor beginning August 15. He eventually did go to work for Sam Jones, but not until August 25 because of accident-related symptoms. Mr. Doe's new rate of pay is $12.50 per hour and he continues to work forty-hour weeks. The wages that my client could have earned from August 15 through August 24 are additional damages attributable to the accident. Mr. Jones will confirm that he had an opening for Mr. Doe on August 15. If my client had been healthy on August 15, he would have gone to work for Mr. Jones on that date. From August 15 through August 24, there were eight (8) work days, or sixty-four hours at $12.50 per hour or $800 in gross lost wages. Total lost wages from both employers are $1,160.

Mr. Doe required thirteen (13) stitches to close a vertical wound in his forehead. The scar is highly visible and 5.2 centimeters in length. A more detailed description of the wound is appended to Dr. Howard Fine's letter to me dated September 13, 1996. It is too early to know if a scar revision is in my client's best interest because the scar will not be mature for about one year. If scar revision is appropriate, Dr. Fine projects the cost to be as much as $15,000. We wouldn't expect you to reimburse Mr. Doe at this time for all of the potential scar revision costs in view of the uncertainty that such costs will be incurred. Neither is it appropriate to simply disregard the possibility that my client may incur these costs or that he may be scarred for the rest of his life. If the case can be settled reasonably, taking into consideration all aspects of my client's damages including the scar and the possibility of the scar revision procedure, my client will give you a full release.

Mr. Doe experienced headaches for two to three days after the accident but had no other symptoms of a head injury. He knew he had problems with his ribs right away. He suffered an abrasion without a lot of bleeding on his right rib cage which later turned "black and blue." Apparently, his ribs were not cracked but badly bruised. The pain that came with bruised ribs was excruciating, especially when Mr. Doe sneezed or coughed. He was sensitive to bumps when riding in his truck. His sleep was impaired during the time that his ribs were sensitive. The pain that my client experienced when he re-injured his ribs on the job on August 10 was traumatic for him. The medical records reflect an emergency trip to the hospital for Mr. Doe in order to suture the wound in his forehead and to x-ray for fractures in his neck, back and shoulders. The x-rays were negative.

I am enclosing the following medical bills which relate to my client's injuries:

1. Main Street Hospital (Dr. Laine Johnson)	$ 389.00
2. Main Street Hospital (emergency services)	594.00
3. Oak Hollow Imaging	55.00
4. Richard Boston, MD	53.00
5. Howard Fine, MD	106.00

In view of the foregoing medical bills, lost wages, and the possibility of substantial additional medical bills associated with the scar revision procedure, I would be willing to settle this claim for $10,000 to $15,000.

Please call me after you have reviewed this package.

Yours truly,

XYZ

Enclosures

Date

Ms. Nancy Johnson
USAA Property and Casualty Insurance
____
____

RE: Claim #000 00000
Insured – Carol Smith
Claimant – Jane Doe

Dear Ms. Johnson:

I represent Jane Doe in connection with the above-referenced claim which arises out of an automobile accident that occurred on September 30, 1995 in Albuquerque, New Mexico. Ms. Doe was a passenger in your insured's vehicle. My client is entitled to reimbursement under the medical payment coverage of your insured's policy as well as the liability provisions of your policy.

With respect to the medical payment benefits, I understand that you have paid a few hundred dollars to date. An accounting of what you have paid would be appreciated. Accident-related medical bills, totaling $4,140.09 are enclosed for your review and payment.

LIABILITY

Insofar as liability is concerned, Ms. Smith failed to yield the right of way to the driver of another vehicle as she pulled out of a driveway onto San Antonio in Albuquerque. The accident report reflects that your insured "cut directly in front of" the other vehicle which "had the right of way." There were no other contributing factors to the accident.

The cause of the accident, as set forth in the police report, is consistent with Ms. Doe's recollection concerning why the accident took place. As I have indicated, she was a passenger in the front seat. As your insured pulled out of the driveway onto San Antonio, she was focused more on her conversation with my client than she was on driving. As a result, she was looking to her right at Ms. Doe as she pulled into the intersection, rather than at the oncoming traffic which was rapidly approaching from her left.

My client was not restrained at the time of the accident because Ms. Smith's vehicle did not have functional seat belts. It may be that such failure represents an independent basis of liability. Ms. Doe was looking at your insured as she also observed the oncoming vehicle approach while Ms. Smith pulled out into the intersection. My client's head was thus rotated to the left at the moment of impact. We believe the oncoming vehicle was traveling at approximately the posted speed limit, 40 mph. The trauma to Ms. Smith's vehicle caused Ms. Doe's head to impact the door of the vehicle, raising a considerable "lump" on the side of her head. She was transported by ambulance from the scene of the accident to a local hospital.

DAMAGES

Ms. Doe's injuries are summarized by Dr. Dan Johnson of the Boulder Medical Center as follows: 1) cervical strain; 2) lumbar strain; 3) right shoulder strain; 4) right elbow contusion, possible strain; 5) some symptoms suggested accident-related depression.

My client had experienced no previous neck or back injuries.

For months after the accident, Ms. Doe experienced migraine headaches, neck stiffness, neck tenderness, fatigue, anxiety, irritability and tinnitus. She experienced the onset of low back pain immediately after the accident. The cervical pain did not come on until several days later.

The quality of my client's life was and continues to be adversely impacted by her accident-related injuries. For instance, she had been restricted to one hour of standing due to pain. She had to use pain killers for relief. The pain with which she had to live impaired her physical performance. During her convalescence, Ms. Doe experienced pain twenty-five percent (25%) to fifty percent (50%) of the time she was awake. She would lift heavy weights but only with pain. She could travel but it caused pain. She could participate sexually but it created pain.

Ms. Doe continues to experience intermittent headaches and stiffness but they tend to be relatively minor. Maintenance adjustments or physical therapy are indicated to minimize the impact of the continuing symptoms as my client continues on the road to recovery.

At the time of the accident, my client had been working at Desert Island Resort as the special events manager where she had been employed since April of 1995. She was accustomed to working six days per week, 55 to 60 hours each week. Her annual gross income was about $32,000. She missed four days of work as a direct result of accident-related symptoms.

More significant, however, is the evidence that Ms. Doe lost her job as a result of her apparent loss of energy brought on by the accident-related injuries. Her job performance was dramatically impacted by the accident. Her struggle with fatigue and irritability in the face of the demands of her job was observed by her supervisor and ultimately the reason for her separation from employment. For months after her termination from the Desert Island Resort, my client and her husband had to make do financially with what he was able to earn and savings they had accumulated. Although Ms. Doe has not yet found comparable employment, we recognize her duty to mitigate this aspect of her damages by seeking and finding other similar work. If this case can be settled, we would expect two months of lost income as reasonable compensation for this element of her damages.

Relevant medical records and billing statements enclosed. As I have indicated above, the cost of future maintenance care is an aspect of my client's damages to be considered.

CONCLUSION

I have attempted to demonstrate the extent to which the quality of my client's life has been adversely impacted for the greater part of a year because of the accident. I should mention that, in weighing such subjective losses, my client is an attractive and likable individual who would make a sympathetic witness on her own behalf.

A jury verdict or arbitration award could reasonably lie in the range from $30,000 to $50,000. I have my client's authorization to settle the liability portion of her claim for $30,000. I would hope that, in the interest of compromise and to avoid the uncertainty, expense and time demands of litigation, we will settle this matter for that amount.

Please call me after your review with any questions in order to bring this matter to conclusion.

Yours truly,

XYZ

Date

Ms. Martha Bennett
CNT Insurance Companies
____
____

RE: CNT Claim #
Claimant: John Doe
CNT Insured: Jane Smith

Dear Ms. Bennett:

I am writing in the hope that the above claim can be settled. You may recall that this claim arises out of an automobile accident that occurred on January 21, 1998 in Castle View, Arizona. Your insured driver is Jane Smith. I represent John Doe and his wife, Joyce.

BACKGROUND

Mr. Doe was positioned to make a left-hand turn in his compact-sized 1980 Datsun sedan when he was hit by Ms. Smith. Your insured was traveling at about 55 mph when he rear-ended Mr. Doe. Ms. Smith was driving a 3/4 ton 1993 Ford pick up truck.

LIABILITY

It's my understanding that you've conceded liability. Ms. Smith indicated, in so many words, that she simply wasn't paying attention to where she was going at the time of the collision. I am not aware of any considerations to suggest that your insured is other than 100% at fault for this accident and Mr. Doe's related injuries.

Ms. Smith was cited for a violation of ARS sec. 28-701(A), driving at a speed that is greater than reasonable and prudent.[1] A copy of the traffic complaint is enclosed for your reference. Our public records investigation reflects that Ms. Smith pleaded guilty to the charge.

[1] ARS sec. 28-701(A): "A person shall not drive a vehicle on a highway at a speed greater than is reasonable and prudent under the circumstances, conditions and actual and potential hazards then existing. A person shall control the speed of a vehicle as necessary to avoid colliding with any object, person, vehicle or other conveyance on, entering or adjacent to the highway in compliance with legal requirements and the duty of all persons to exercise reasonable care for the protection of others."

DAMAGES

What we have is a high speed rear-end collision. Ms. Smith was traveling at about 55 mph or 75 feet per second. Your insured's large pick up truck demolished Mr. Doe's smaller Datsun. Photographs of the Datsun, after the accident, are enclosed. After impact, my client's vehicle spun counter-clockwise out of control into the eastbound lane of traffic. Fortunately, there was no eastbound traffic to further complicate this accident or add to Mr. Doe's injuries.

Mr. Doe had no reason to anticipate the impending collision. He therefore had no opportunity to brace for the accident. When he was hit, Mr. Doe's head was rotated to the left in the direction of his anticipated turn. In addition to the severity of the impact, the fact that Mr. Doe's head was rotated and that he was unaware of the impending collision are accident mechanisms which explain the more serious symptoms experienced by him as a result of his whiplash.

Mr. Doe's injuries included a compound fracture of his right thumb and cervical strain. The thumb required surgery as described by Dr. Peter Thomas' report. The cervical strain required several months of physical therapy. All of the relevant medical records and bills are enclosed. A brief analysis of each of my client's more serious injuries may be useful in coming to terms.

CERVICAL STRAIN

During much of my client's recovery from his cervical spine injury, he was nagged by headaches. The headaches were more severe during the end of the day. In the morning, he suffered from neck stiffness. He would wear a cervical collar as he needed to. He's also taken medication as necessary to keep the symptoms under control. Some of the symptoms continue to this day especially after extended sitting or driving.

My client's medical records and bills from Carol Jace of Valley Center Physical Rehabilitation are enclosed. He underwent about two months of physical rehabilitation at considerable expense ($1,047.50).

Although Mr. Doe's cervical spine is now stable, he's worried about his susceptibility to re-injury and arthritis, both of which are genuine concerns.

Approximately $2,000 of the enclosed medical bills are allocated to Mr. Doe's cervical spine injury. If we were to settle the neck injury separately, the claim would be worth $5,000 to $7,000.

FRACTURED THUMB

Please refer to the records from Omega Orthopedics by Dr. Peter Thomas concerning Mr. Doe's fractured thumb. My client underwent an open reduction with the installation of various hardware to repair his broken thumb.

Mr. Doe's thumb is now stable, but he has suffered a permanent loss of function of the thumb. He has sustained what Dr. Thomas describes as ankylosed ("stiffness of union of a joint by disease or surgery") thumb. Simply stated, he can't bend his right thumb.

Mr. Doe can no longer perform many routine tasks with his right hand because of the loss of function in his thumb. He finds himself having to use his left hand for tasks which he's performed all his life with his right hand. He has a difficult time using certain tools. Common tasks as simple as buttoning clothing are now problematic. The thumb is apparently one of those limbs that we take for granted until it no longer functions as it should.

Dr. Thomas' letter dated April 28 concerning my client's thumb problem is enclosed for your reference. He describes Mr. Doe's permanent impairment of the hand at approximately 20%. That functional loss translates into a 3% limitation of the whole man.

Jury verdict research indicates that for finger fractures, including the thumb, when there is permanent impairment and $5,000 to $7,500 in medical bills, the adjusted "basic injury value" is $41,160.

Adding the $6,000 in restitution for my client's cervical spine injury to the $41,160 in restitution for his permanent thumb injury, we come to $47,160 as total compensation for my client's accident-related losses.

Please contact me after you've reviewed these materials to discuss a final resolution of this matter.

Yours truly,

XYZ

Enclosures

INDEX

ORDER FORM

Fax orders: 928-284-2191 Send this form.

Telephone Orders: 928-284-2190 No credit cards please.

E-mail Orders: fitzlaw@sedona.net • *www.autojustice.net*

Postal Orders: Courtney Publishing, Doug Fitzpatrick,
49 Bell Rock Plaza, Suite A, Sedona, AZ 86351

☐ Please send *Auto Claims Without Attorneys, A Guide to Settlement.*

I understand that I may return the book for a full refund for any reason, no questions asked.

☐ Please send a wholesale price list.

****

Name:
____

Address:
____
____

City: ____________________ State: ________Zip:____________

Telephone: __________ e-mail address: ______________________

****

Please remit payment by check or money order for:
$12.95 plus $3.00 shipping and handling.

Thank you.

"If you think you can or you can't, you're always right."

-- Henry Ford

"Great works are performed not by strength but by perseverance."

-- Samuel Johnson